THE RAILWAYS OF KEYNSHAM

Featuring Fry's Chocolate Passenger and Freight Operations

by
Russell Leitch

THE RAILWAY CORRESPONDENCE AND TRAVEL SOCIETY

© RCTS 1997

ISBN 090 1115 827

Published by Railway Correspondence and Travel Society
11 Suffield Close, Long Stratton, Norfolk, NR15 2JL

COVER DESIGN BY JOHN COLLINS

Printed and typeset by MFP Design & Print, Manchester

Cover Photo
The classic early British Railways era at Keynsham. The number of 2-6-2T 5526 goes into the train spotters' books as it calls with the Saturdays Only 3.35p.m Bristol - Westbury on 30th July 1960.   *Author*

Inside Front Cover
The first timetable from 31st August 1840.

GWR broad gauge 2-4-0 formerly Bristol and Exeter Railway No 6. Probably at Bristol Bath Road.

National Railway Museum, York.

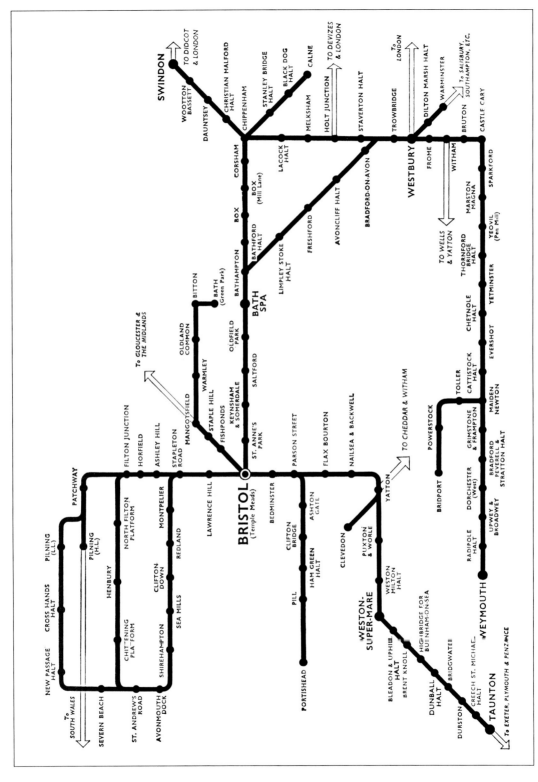

This diagrammatic map appeared in the timetable booklets published by British Rail in connection with the dieselisation of local Bristol services in 1959 (see Chapter 5). The branch from Bristol to Frome was omitted because it was still worked wholly by steam.

INTRODUCTION

Sometimes it is good to take a magnifying glass and look at an already familiar subject in greater detail. One is almost always surprised by the discovery of new aspects, new angles, new details, and above all new depth, not before appreciated. The difference made by greater depth of appreciation can be as great as between three dimensions or two, or between feeling or merely seeing.

This principle applies to our railway interest too, in my opinion. I believe that too often we try to absorb masses of detail about a broad subject in the railway world, yet fail to appreciate the full significance. (Rather like not seeing the trees for the wood, I suppose.) History is easy to read, but difficult to feel. Only a very capable tour guide can bring history vividly back to life.

In this book we have such a guide. We are invited not merely to study the bold facts and figures of the railways around Keynsham, but to feel the atmosphere of the place, including the social environment in which the railway operated. There are rich opportunities for the imagination to recreate the scene in full colour, all the more tempting because whereas in most places one would have to imagine the heavy smells of smoke and fog, here one might imagine the smell of chocolate.

Here, then is an opportunity to take a stroll through history, or, better still, to settle comfortably in an armchair, transport it to Keynsham, and watch the cavalcade. All the necessary detail is there, from the first coming of the railway, the arrival of Fry's, the creation of Fry's own railway infrastructure, the freight and passenger services provided for the factory, the growth years, decline, threat of closure, rationalisation, and above all a happy ending, with a buoyant present day scene (a new service to Filton Abbey Wood added recently) and good prospects for the future of the area.

Russell Leitch can claim 70 years of interest in railways generally, 50 of them in the Bristol area. Who better to take us on this fascinating trip to the past? Our warmest thanks are due to him for undertaking the huge task which now makes such a trip possible.

Hugh Gould
Hon President
RCTS
January 1997

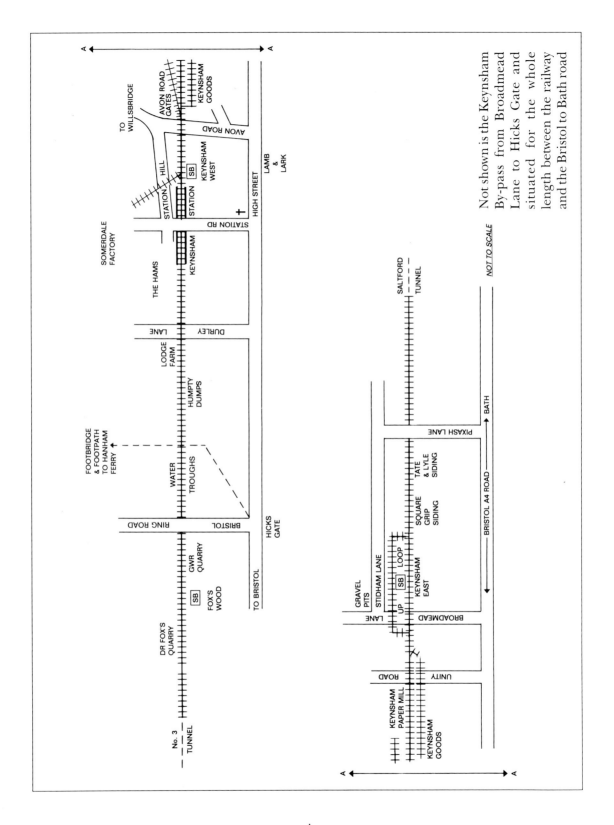

Not shown is the Keynsham By-pass from Broadmead Lane to Hicks Gate and situated for the whole length between the railway and the Bristol to Bath road

vi

KEYNSHAM'S RAILWAYS
AND
THE FRY'S CHOCOLATE TRAINS

CONTENTS

Keynsham Station in the 1930s with an up freight passing through. Note the then new Station Road bridge and platform awnings at the far end of the station. The footbridge is now preserved on the South Devon Railway at Buckfastleigh.

Lens of Sutton

PREFACE

Relocation of work in 1950 brought me to live in Keynsham, whereas my office was seven miles away in Bath. A weekly season ticket between the two stations was modestly priced at 39 pence in to-day's money. Because of my regular use of the railway I came to be well known in the town as an "authority" on railways, which I certainly was not, except that perhaps an authority on the timetable.

So it came about that back in 1977 the Secretary of the Keynsham and Saltford Local History Society came across a booklet recording the history of the Bath Railway Society. Therein was a reference to an illustrated talk I gave on the railway between Bristol and Bath. That prompted him to ask me to give a similar talk to the Local History Society except that "We don't want pictures of engines and trains!" At that time I knew next to nothing about the history of the line, but somewhat foolhardily I agreed to do the talk. The saving grace was that I had six months to do something about it. That opened up for me a whole new vista of Public Record Offices, Reference Libraries and a whole range of other sources of information. By just asking I managed to get a personally conducted tour of the rapidly decaying offices and Board Room within the original 1840 Temple Meads station, together with the Bristol and Exeter Railway building of 1854 on the opposite side of the station approach road. That helped considerably when the time came to give my illustrated talk.

I also possessed a whole stack of GWR magazines, almost complete from 1898 through to 1947, which I had bought for £4 during a railway clearance sale, purchased as a long term investment, but hardly ever opened. (I always buy the wrong things. If only I had invested the money in an engine nameplate, still then available for that sort of money). Those magazines provided a mine of information.

In my opening address to the Society I told them that the task of preparing for the evening proved to be so fascinating that I might well continue with my research and go on to

publication. So, here we are nearly twenty years later.

Of all those who helped me in the early days, my especial thanks must go to Tom Richards, together with his book "Was your Grandfather a Railwayman". That book introduced me to the Public Record Office at Kew and helped me to find my way around. Then there is the reference section of the Bristol Central Library who have answered a multitude of questions, and when unable to come up with the answer, have provided valuable pointers as to where the answer may be found.

For the chapter setting out the early history of the Somerdale factory of J.S. Fry & Co Ltd. I am indebted to Mrs Helen Davies, the Librarian and Archivist at Cadbury Ltd, Bournville, to Mr J.F. Reed, Site Services Manager at Somerdale and to Mr John Collins for artwork. I am grateful for the contributions made by the relatives of former station masters, the late Miss E. Webb (daughter), Mr A.F. Sparey (son) and Mrs A. Frere (the late Mr N.R. Bartrum's daughter). Then there is Mrs Margaret Whitehead, the archivist to the Keynsham and Saltford Local History Society. I must also acknowledge the support given and encouragement of fellow enthusiasts, not least the members of the Bristol Branch of the Railway Correspondence and Travel Society (RCTS).

Within the narrative there are two significant dates to be taken into account. With the Summer 1964 timetable British Rail introduced the 24 hour clock notation, and on 15th February 1971 there came the decimalisation of the currency.

Prior to the introduction of the 24 hour clock it was not customary to use four digits when documenting times, e.g. 8.8 rather than 8.08. Historic accuracy has been followed in the text, though tabular presentations employ the more modern system for clarity.

Cognisance needs to be taken in the change in nomenclature of motive power. In steam days they were engines and they dwelt in engine sheds. Now, with diesels and electrics they are locomotives.

Postcript. During the 1960s Keynsham rose to national fame when Horace Batchelor advertised services as a football pools expert on Radio Luxembourg. Those who were so minded to part with their money were invited to send it to an address in K E Y N S H A M, the spelling carefully repeated a second time.

Russell Leitch
Keynsham
January 1997

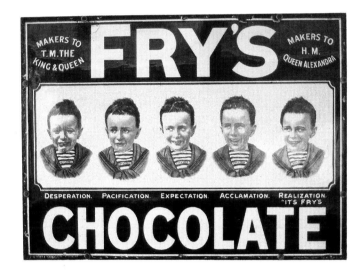

1. The first five years 1840-1845

On 31st August 1840, five years to the day from when King William IV gave his Royal Assent to the Act of Parliament for the construction of the Great Western Railway, the first train left Temple Meads station a few minutes after its booked time of eight o'clock, hauled by the engine *Fire Ball*. It comprised three elegant first class carriages and five second class. It called at Keynsham on route to Bath. However, the first train from Keynsham to Bristol was 43 minutes late. In British Rail speak it was caused by "operational difficulties in the Bath area." There would not have been an apology for "any inconvenience caused." In truth, the delay was caused by "Some deficiency in a wheel of one of the second class carriages."[1] There was further delay at Twerton because of a fire alarm. That proved to be unfounded, but there were sparks which caused alarm among the passengers, and that because one of the wheels was not quite clear of the carriage and grated against it. The newspaper report concluded by saying "The same thing happened several times during the day with the same unimportant result."[1]

The four engines said to have been assembled in Saltford tunnel were all in use on that first day, viz *Fire Ball, Arrow, Lynx* and *Meriden*.

Fares from
      Keynsham to Bristol were:
      1/6 (7½p) first class 9d (4p) second.
      Keynsham to Bath
      2/- (10p) first class 1/- (5p) second

There were no return fares. What did the passengers get for their money? The Bristol Mirror put it this way: "In the short space of twelve miles (between Bristol and Bath) every aspect of work occurs: there are viaducts, bridges, deep cuttings, high embankments and tunnels, so that in this brief and pleasant trip there is every species of novelty to gratify curiosity."

The same newspaper, on 29th August, raised another issue of considerable importance, when in a leading article it stated:

"We think it not amiss to add, at a time when public attention is painfully excited by dreadful casualties on other lines, that although nearly two million passengers have passed over that part of the Great Western line already open to the public (by then Paddington to Farringdon Road) not one individual has lost his life, or any serious accident occurred. This is in no great measure to be attributed to the width of gauge which renders it all but impossible for carriages to run off the rails, and which, whilst it is productive to a vast superiority of speed, ensures also a superiority of a point of infinitely more importance - safety."

Sekon, in his History of the Great Western Railway (1895) put it this way:

"Carriages had six wheels and were therefore safer than narrow gauge with four wheels if an axle broke or a wheel came off".

The Great Western maintained its proud boast for safety right to the end of its days.

The first timetable provided ten trains each way between Bristol and Bath of which six called at Keynsham. On Sundays there were only four trains, and there was a nine hour gap between 9am and 6pm. (See inside front cover) During the first few years there were frequent changes to the timetable, notably when through trains commenced to run between Paddington and Bristol in 1841.

Within the first week of service the Bristol Mirror was reporting complaints (in the plural) concerning the lack of a train at four o'clock from Bath which would allow passengers to get back to Bristol in time for dinner at the customary hour of five. Not exactly a complaint, but the same newspaper also observed that there was insufficient time when the train stopped at Keynsham "to step out and have a glass with the coachman."

The takings for the first eighteen days of service are set out overleaf. Two things stand

---

[1]*Felix Farley's Bristol Journal.*

Keynsham Revenue - The First Eighteen Days

	1840	BRISTOL £	s	d	KEYNSHAM £	s	d	BATH £	s	d	TOTAL £	s	d	PASSENGERS
Monday	31st August	223.	17.	1 ½	21.	14.	0	230.	19.	0	476.	10.	1 ½	5880
Tuesday	1st September	131.	11.	7 ½	9.	19.	4 ½	122.	10.	6	264.	1.	6	3361
Wednesday	2nd	96.	18.	3	5.	18.	9	92.	17.	0	195.	14.	0	2390
Thursday	3rd	97.	17.	3	4.	14.	9	90.	6.	9	192.	18.	9	2361
Friday	4th	69.	8.	6	4.	17.	5	65.	0.	0	139.	5.	11	1673
Saturday	5th	65.	12.	11	5.	18.	8	72.	17.	6	144.	9.	1	1789
Sunday	6th	67.	13.	8	16.	13.	7	68.	10.	9	152.	18.	0	2217 ½
Monday	7th	124.	1.	5	10.	15.	11	127.	1.	3	261.	18.	7	3336 ½
Tuesday	8th	127.	10.	8	6.	8.	11	129.	1.	6	263.	1.	1	3193 ½
Wednesday	9th	79.	9.	9 ½	5.	13.	4	77.	19.	0	163.	2.	1 ½	1999 ½
Thursday	10th	121.	6.	11 ½	6.	12.	5	115.	19.	3	243.	18.	7 ½	2931 ½
Friday	11th	87.	15.	6	4.	4.	9	88.	11.	9	180.	12.	0	2100 ½
Saturday	12th	71.	1.	0 ½	4.	6.	8	72.	2.	9	147.	10.	5 ½	1758 ½
Sunday	13th	99.	6.	6	13.	16.	2	99.	11.	3	212.	13.	11	2890
Monday	14th	77.	0.	2	6.	10.	5	76.	6.	9	159.	17.	4	2039
Tuesday	15th	109.	19.	1	6.	0.	9	111.	18.	6	227.	18.	4	2734
Wednesday	16th	60.	8.	4 ½	2.	18.	2	58.	10.	0	121.	16.	6 ½	1463
Thursday	17th	108.	14.	3 ½	5.	11.	8	107.	19.	7 ½	222.	5.	7	2709
		1819.	**13.**	**1 ½**	**142.**	**15.**	**8 ½**	**1808.**	**3.**	**1 ½**	**3770.**	**11.**	**11 ½**	**46826 ½**

out as far as Keynsham is concerned. First, it is quite obvious that Keynsham was the poor relation. Even on the best days the takings did no better than approximate to 25% of the worst days at Bristol or Bath. Secondly, apart from the novelty of the 31st August, the best days takings at Keynsham were both Sundays. Thus, the dire warnings from the pulpit of the heinous sin of Sabbath breaking went unheeded. However, it has to be recognised that the bulk of the takings related to passengers from Bristol and Bath purchasing tickets for the return journey.

(As a side issue, older readers may like to test their long lost expertise in £sd arithmetic. Younger readers should try and work out how it was done.) 12d equalled one shilling and there were twenty shillings to the £. See also appendix F.

On Wednesday, 23rd September 1840, less than a month after the railway was opened, there was a "Shocking Railway Accident" on the line. Robert Rudell, aged 80, was struck by the five o'clock train from Bristol to Bath whilst crossing the line in pursuit of his avocations at the gravel pits at Keynsham. The gravel pits were situated at the Broadmead Lane end of Stidham Lane.

The more complete account of the tragedy appears in Felix Farley's Bristol Journal, where the report points somewhat conclusively to suicide. The train engine was *Stag*, newly delivered from Sharp Roberts & Co., Manchester only a week or two prior to the accident.

By the end of September 1840, the railway was advertising a parcels service. Parcels could be booked at the railway stations at Bristol and Bath, and also at the Railway Office in Corn Street, Bristol, for conveyance to Bath, Bristol or Keynsham. The charge was one shilling where the weight did not exceed 28lbs, 1/6d (7½p) when not exceeding 56lbs. There was an extra sixpence (2½p) for every additional quarter cwt. The charge was inclusive of carriage, porterage and delivery. Strangely, parcels could be conveyed to Keynsham, but there was no advertised facility in the reverse direction. Four deliveries were made each day - a truly lavish service. That would have caused no problem at Keynsham where the porter could easily nip around the village in the hourly

BRISTOL AND BATH.

Horses, Carriages, &c. will be conveyed by Railway between BRISTOL and BATH Stations on and after the 16th of December. The SALTFORD and TWERTON Stations will also be Opened for the conveyance of Passengers, Parcels, &c.

HOURS OF DEPARTURE, REGULATED BY BRISTOL TIME, until the whole Line shall be Opened. DAILY, (EXCEPTING SUNDAYS).

UP From Bristol	Departure from				Arrives at Bath	DOWN From Bath	Departure from				Arrives at Bristol
	Bristol	Keynsham	Saltford	Twerton			Bath	Twerton	Saltford	Keynsham	
To	h. m.	h.m.	h.m.	h.m.	h. m.	To	h. m.	h. m.	h. m.	h. m.	h. m.
BATH A.M.	7. 0	....	7.15	......	7. 25	BRISTOL A.M.	8. 0	. .	8.10	. . .	8.25
,, ,,	9. 0	9.10	......	......	9. 25	,, ,,	10. 0	. .	. .	10.15	10.25
,, ,,	10. 0	....	......	......	10. 23	,, ,,	11. 0	11. 4	. .	. . .	11.25
,, ,,	11. 0	11.10	11.16	11.24	11. 30	,, ,,	12. 0	. .	12.10	. . .	12.25
,, ,,	12. 0	....	......	......	12. 23	,, P.M.	1. 0	. .	. .	1.15	1.25
,, P.M.	2. 0	2.10	......	......	2. 25	,, ,,	3. 0	3. 4	. .	. . .	3.25
,, ,,	3. 0	....	......	3.20	3. 25	,, ,,	4. 0	. .	. .	4.15	4.25
,, ,,	4. 0	....	4.15	......	4. 25	,, ,,	5. 0	. .	. .	. . .	5.23
,, ,,	5. 0	5.10	......	......	5. 25	,, ,,	6. 0	6. 4	6.12	6.18	6.30
,, ,,	6. 0	....	......	6.20	6. 25	,, ,,	7. 0	. .	. .	. . .	7.23
,, ,,	8. 0	8.10	......	......	8. 25	,, ,,	9. 0	. .	. .	9.15	9.25

ON SUNDAYS.

		h.m.	h.m.	h. m.	h. m.	h. m.			h. m.	h. m.	h. m.	h. m.	h. m.
,, A.M.	8. 0	8.10	......	8.21	8.26	,, A.M.	9. 0	9. 4	......	9.16	9.26
,, ,,	9. 0	9.10	9.16	......	9.26	,, ,,	10. 0	......	10.10	10.16	10.26
,, P.M.	2. 0	2.10	2.16	2.24	2.30	,, P.M.	3. 0	3. 4	3.18	3.18	3.30
,, ,,	5. 0	5.10	5.16	5.24	5.30	,, ,,	6. 0	6. 4	6.18	6.18	6.30
,, ,,	8. 0	8.10	8.16	8.24	8.30	,, ,,	9. 0	9. 4	9.18	9.18	9.30

Train Bills, and further Particulars, may be had at the Railway Offices and Stations on Tuesday the 15th Instant. By Order of the Directors,

CHAS. A. SAUNDERS, THOMAS OSLER, } Secretaries.

11th December, 1840.

SECOND TIMETABLE - Wednesday 16th December 1840 (The stations at Saltford and Twerton opened on that date). Except for the 10.10, all the Saltford down train Sunday timings were misprints.

The first Royal Train passed through Keynsham on 19th July 1843, conveying HRH Prince Albert to and from Bristol in connection the launch of the SS *Great Britain*.

Finally, it is worthy of note that when the railway first arrived in Bristol, local time was eleven minutes later than London time. From the beginning, all railways worked throughout to London time so that, in due course, Greenwich Mean Time, as it now is, became standard throughout the land.

We will now digress and consider the plight of third class passengers. To be blunt - they were simply not wanted. It would appear that the Great Western made no provision for such undesirables until the line was opened throughout from Paddington to Bristol in 1841 Then the following note appeared in the timetable: "The goods train passengers will be conveyed in uncovered trucks; only 14lbs of luggage is allowed to each, all excess is charged at the usual rate for passengers luggage." The railway servants of those days would have been heartless and stuck rigidly to the rules so that every pound of excess would have been charged. The railway station was a primitive version of a modern airport check-in procedure

During 1841 and 1842 there were only two goods trains each day between Paddington and Bristol. One left Paddington at the most inconvenient hour of 4.30am, but did not arrive in Bristol until 1.55pm. The other ran by night. As far as it is known the goods trains did not call at Keynsham, presumably because there was no goods yard.

By 1844 the plight of goods train passengers had become a national scandal. That caused Mr Gladstone to pilot through Parliament an Act for the Amelioration of Third Class Passengers. The Act required each railway to provide:

"At least one train each day to call at all stations
The fare to be no more than one penny per mile
Covered carriages with seats to be provided
A minimum speed of 12mph including stoppages."

Very quickly the trains were dubbed "Parliamentary trains" and they survived as such on some minor railways into the 20th Century. The GWR responded to the Act by constructing six covered carriages, with seats, but no windows. The following year they relented by providing one small window and one oil lamp per carriage. They also relented by allowing third class passengers to take up to 56lbs of luggage free of charge - the same as for second class passengers.

Within the spirit of the Act the GWR provided one train each way, every day including Sundays, between Paddington and Bristol. It called at every station on the line and was timed as follows.[4]

Paddington	dep 7am
Keynsham	arr 4.2pm
Keynsham	dep 9.50am
Paddington	arr 7pm

The average speed was near enough $12\frac{1}{2}$ mph.

The timetable also quoted another train in each direction at night, available to third class passengers, leaving Paddington down at 9.30pm and Bristol up at 10pm. They did not call at Keynsham or at a number of other intermediate stations and, therefore, they were not Parliamentary trains. Nevertheless, the overall speed of the two trains was still in the region of $12\frac{1}{2}$ mph. McDermott in his History of the Great Western Railway said that until 1875 there was only the legal minimum of one general third class train in each direction on the main line and branches and that would have been the position at Keynsham. The statement needs qualification as third class passengers were admitted to other trains, including some fast ones where there was competition with other railways.

How did the stage coaches fare after the arrival of the railway? Sekon in his history of the Great Western Railway, published in 1895, states that to meet the competition a half hourly service of coaches was put on the road between Bristol and Bath. That compared with an hourly frequency by rail, but of course, the

---

[4]*Great Western Railway Advertiser 29th January 1845*

trains were much quicker. A contemporary report in the Bristol Mirror quoted 80 coaches each day between Bristol and Bath.

Percy Sims, in his History of Saltford Village, includes the following delightful passage:

"Several stage coaches have announced they will still continue to run, and although Jarvey's face was less cheery than of yore, he proposes that it will be a long time before the last of his race will be seen on the Bath Road, as many persons will prefer glorifying in a set of smoking bays to being whistled along by a boiling pot of water."

R.C. Tombs, one time Postmaster of Bristol, said "One coach obstinately held its ground, in spite of the railway, and continued to carry passengers from Bristol to London at the rate of one penny per mile until 1843."[5] No doubt, that coach called for custom at the Lamb and Lark Hotel.[6] But realism soon set in. Pigot's Directory of Somerset for 1842 noted that coaches to and from Bristol and Bath passed through Keynsham several times during the day. Ten years later, Slater's Directory of Somerset 1852-53, noted that Loader's coach from Bath to Clifton called at the Lamb and Lark every morning at eleven and returned in the evening at half past five. Loader must surely have been the last survivor of a one time thriving trade which had been killed off by the railway.

Joseph Leech visited Keynsham in 1844 and published in the Bristol Times on 4th October of that year his experience en route. The article was part of an ongoing series in the newspaper entitled "The Rural Rides of a Bristol Churchgoer". His comments concerning the demeanour of some railway passengers does not seem to have changed much from that day to this.

"Most persons visiting Keynsham would have taken eighteen pence in their pocket and a place in a second class carriage. But I was born before an inch of 'permanent way' was laid down, and when I get the turnpike road, with leafy hedges and green fields on both sides of me, I have no wish to be shot through dark tunnels like a pea through a peashooter. My time is not so precious that I cannot afford to loiter an additional hour on the way; nor is it a loss either, for you generally meet, or rather met, with some conversable creature in a stage coach, from which you departed a trifle wiser; it might be on Mangel Worzel, or it might be on the Elgin Marbles. Now you have time to pick up nothing in a railroad carriage but a heart complaint; you get in, a look around for a colloquial face in an absolute company, and if you are fortunate enough to find one amongst persons who appear cast iron, like the permanent way, beneath them, you clear your throat, give a preliminary cough or two, and you have just time to make a remark on the salubrity of the season when the train stops, the door is unlocked by a man in Lincoln green, who shouts 'Who's for Nailsea, or Nottingham' as the case may be, and your vis-a-vis alights and your gossip is nipped in the bud.

The road to Keynsham, though pleasant, fortunately for the reader presents little to reflect upon. The only incident which merits a special record is, perhaps, the fact of John Bunyan [his horse] having been frightened by the up train, just at that point where the railway approaches the turnpike close to Keynsham. I was balancing myself in the saddle, repeating part of Keble's Christian year, when John with his regular foot-fall, kept time to the cadence of the verse when 'whirr!' - out from the side of the hill shot the bright copper boiler with its train of polished carriages, like a monstrous tea kettle eloping with a string of monstrous tea caddies. John snorted and elevated his tail a little, and then pausing as if deliberating whether he ought to expend any more of his energies on a start. But he took the more sensible course and stood still, although I could perceive he was greatly alarmed. It was evidently the first time he had seen a railroad, and I thought I would endeavour to convince

---

[5]*The Royal Bristol Mail. Published in 1899*

[6]*The Lamb and Lark was a well known hostelry in the Keynsham High Street facing the top of Bath Hill. It was demolished in 1970. The site is now occupied by Ronto's the ladies fashion shop, and by Somerfield Supermarket.*

him of the unreasonableness of his fears; so turning his head in the direction of the still retreating train, and patting him encouragingly on the neck, I told him it was a locomotive engine – an invention of modern science for superseding his species; that it made a great deal of noise, but contrary to the adage, did a great deal of work also. He seemed reassured, and by the time we entered the Lamb and Lark had completely recovered his equanimity."

Note:
Joseph Leech was a very strong supporter of the Established Church and had little time for Dissenters. Possibly, he called his horse John Bunyan as a mark of contempt for Dissenters.

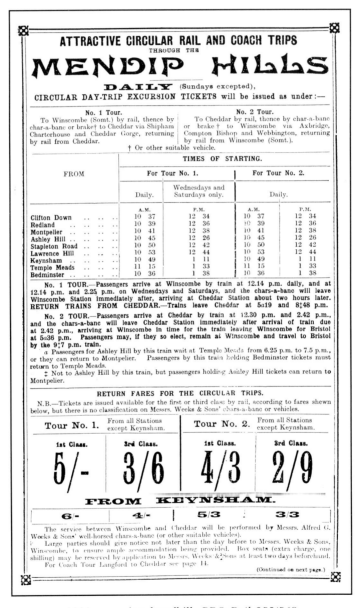

ATTRACTIVE CIRCULAR RAIL AND COACH TRIPS
THROUGH THE
MENDIP HILLS
DAILY (Sundays excepted),
CIRCULAR DAY-TRIP EXCURSION TICKETS will be issued as under :—

No. 1 Tour.	No. 2 Tour.
To Winscombe (Somt.) by rail, thence by char-a-banc or brake† to Cheddar via Shipham Charterhouse and Cheddar Gorge, returning by rail from Cheddar.	To Cheddar by rail, thence by char-a-banc or brake† to Winscombe via Axbridge, Compton Bishop and Webbington, returning by rail from Winscombe (Somt.).

† Or other suitable vehicle.

TIMES OF STARTING.

FROM	For Tour No. 1.		For Tour No. 2.	
	Daily.	Wednesdays and Saturdays only.	Daily.	
	A.M.	P.M.	A.M.	P.M.
Clifton Down	10 37	12 34	10 37	12 34
Redland	10 39	12 36	10 39	12 36
Montpelier	10 41	12 38	10 41	12 38
Ashley Hill	10 45	12 26	10 45	12 26
Stapleton Road	10 50	12 42	10 50	12 42
Lawrence Hill	10 53	12 44	10 53	12 44
Keynsham	10 49	1 11	10 49	1 11
Temple Meads	11 15	1 33	11 15	1 33
Bedminster	10 36	1 38	10 36	1 38

No. 1 TOUR.—Passengers arrive at Winscombe by train at 12.14 p.m. daily, and at 12.14 p.m. and 2.25 p.m. on Wednesdays and Saturdays, and the chars-a-banc will leave Winscombe Station immediately after, arriving at Cheddar Station about two hours later. RETURN TRAINS FROM CHEDDAR.—Trains leave Cheddar at 5a19 and 8‡48 p.m.

No. 2 TOUR.—Passengers arrive at Cheddar by train at 12.30 p.m. and 2.42 p.m., and the chars-a-banc will leave Cheddar Station immediately after arrival of train due at 2.42 p.m., arriving at Winscombe in time for the train leaving Winscombe for Bristol at 5a36 p.m. Passengers may, if they so elect, remain at Winscombe and travel to Bristol by the 9‡7 p.m. train.

a Passengers for Ashley Hill by this train wait at Temple Meads from 6.25 p.m. to 7.5 p.m., or they can return to Montpelier. Passengers by this train holding Bedminster tickets must return to Temple Meads.

‡ Not to Ashley Hill by this train, but passengers holding Ashley Hill tickets can return to Montpelier.

RETURN FARES FOR THE CIRCULAR TRIPS.

N.B.—Tickets are issued available for the first or third class by rail, according to fares shewn below, but there is no classification on Messrs. Weeks & Sons' chars-a-banc or vehicles.

Tour No. 1.	From all Stations except Keynsham.		Tour No. 2.	From all Stations except Keynsham.	
1st Class.	**3rd Class.**		**1st Class.**	**3rd Class.**	
5/-	3/6		4/3	2/9	

FROM KEYNSHAM.

6/-	4/-		5/3	3/3

The service between Winscombe and Cheddar will be performed by Messrs. Alfred G. Weeks & Sons' well-horsed chars-a-banc (or other suitable vehicles).

Large parties should give notice not later than the day before to Messrs. Weeks & Sons, Winscombe, to ensure ample accommodation being provided. Box seats (extra charge, one shilling) may be reserved by application to Messrs. Weeks & Sons at least two days beforehand. For Coach Tour Langford to Cheddar see page 14.

(Continued on next page.)

1911 excursion handbill. *PRO Rail 253/569*

2. Brislington Tunnel to Keynsham

The 11½ mile railway between Bristol and Bath is the most heavily engineered continuous length of railway between Bristol and Paddington. Both Bristol Temple Meads and Bath Spa stations are built on arches as are lengths of the intervening line. There were originally seven tunnels, three of which have been opened out and there are three long embankments, the one at Twerton overlooking the Lower Bristol Road being retained by a substantial stone wall, the embankment at Saltford almost two miles in length, and that crossing The Hams at Keynsham three quarters of a mile. The only significant portion of the line which is at ground level is a short stretch in the vicinity of Pixash Lane, Keynsham. The route was constructed with a ruling gradient of 1 in 1320, or falling at the rate of four feet per mile in the direction of Bristol. The track was at Brunel's broad gauge of 7ft 0¼ins.

Approximately 3¾ miles of the line is included in the Keynsham tithe map of 1841, from Saltford tunnel west portal to the site of the former Fox's Wood signal box. To lay that length of line Brunel had to purchase 68 acres 3 roods and 18 perches of land, of which 54 acres 1 rood and 30 perches were used for the actual railroad.[1] The balance, being mostly odd corners, were let to tenants. 41 acres and 28 perches were exempt from the payment of Great and Small Tithes. On the remainder of the land Brunel still had to pay annual tithe charges of £1 9s 2d (£1·46) to the Duke of Buckingham and Chandos and £2 12s 8d (£2·63) to the Vicar of Keynsham. Some of the tithes payable to the Vicar by Brunel were ridiculously small, for example, 2d (1p) for 27 perches in Broad Mead Pasture and 7d (3p) for 18 perches of withy bed. Nevertheless, from all sources, the Vicar gathered for himself an annual total of £170 5s 0d (£170·25) and that in the days when the Keynsham Baptist Minister was only paid £100 per annum.

Brunel lost no time in getting started on this massive undertaking. Within four days of the passing of the Act of Parliament on 31st August 1835 he was writing to Messrs Osborn and Ward, the lawyers, and to Townsend, the surveyor, requesting that they take steps to clear the land at Brislington so that he could determine the exact course of the line. In a letter to the Directors, dated 18th June 1836, Brunel gave a report which mentioned work already in progress at Saltford. That is confirmed by a stone on an inside wall of the long disused Saltford Battery Mill upon which is engraved the words "Begun diggin the railroad June 11 1836". Initially, progress was quite good as the embankment across the Keynsham Hams was complete by the end of 1837. The disruption caused to the village of Keynsham can be summed up by an 1837 entry in the Minute Book of the Keynsham Baptist Church which reads:

"We cannot but wonder at the long suffering patience of God towards us. The state of society around us is inexpressibly deplorable. Satan seems to have established his seat among us. We have long been considered infamous for immorality, but since the commencement of the Great Western Railway wickedness has greatly increased. Drunkenness, swearing, Sabbath breaking and other vices which generally accompany these are presenting a most alarming aspect and many who used to pay some outward regard to religion have cast off all restraint and have become impudent in their crimes."

By way of contrast, the diary of George Henry Gibbs, a director of the GWR, records that on the 6th December 1837 he spoke to Mr Willis "concerning the propriety of affording the navigators as they approach Bath with some opportunities for religious instruction".

---

[1]30¼ square yards = 1 square rod, pole or perch
40 square rods, poles or perches = 1 rood
4 roods = 1 acre.

Presumably, Bath being a place of Quality, merited something better than that place of ill repute known as Keynsham

Although a short length of line at each end is beyond the Keynsham Parish boundary, for the purpose of this narrative, the stretch of line to be considered is that between the Eastern portal of No 3 tunnel and the Western portal of Saltford Tunnel. No 3 Tunnel is now more usually referred to as either Brislington Tunnel, Fox's Wood Tunnel, or The Long Tunnel. (No 1 tunnel was west of St Anne's Park and opened out in 1887, and No 2 tunnel is the short tunnel east of St Anne' Park.) The work on No 3 tunnel was not completed until November 1839.

Contract 2B was let to one William Ranger to cover construction of the line east of No 3 tunnel. His progress was unsatisfactory, and the Bristol Committee on Works records:[2]

7th April 1838   Notice to be served on Wm Ranger that the Company will proceed with and complete contracts 1B and 2B unless carried on to the Directors' satisfaction within seven days.

10th July 1838   The Resident Engineer to be instructed to proceed with the works lately carried out by Mr Ranger on contracts 1B and 2B, also to provide an inventory of plant and materials not provided by the Company.

Mr Ranger took umbrage and went to Court. Proceedings dragged on in Chancery until 1855, sometime after the plaintiff had departed this life. McIntosh took over the contract in addition to his other contracts. He also eventually became a plaintiff in Chancery, faring much worse for his case lasted until 1865 and he never lived to see the outcome. The only true winners were the lawyers.

Construction of the first half mile after leaving No 3 tunnel was particularly difficult. The railway is high above the River Avon with very little foothold. In order to obtain the required foothold, it was necessary to divert the river to the extent of half its width. Furthermore, a massive arched retaining wall was constructed, not only to support the railway, but also to protect it from sliding into the river. The necessity for such a course of action was evidenced by a landslide which carried away into the river much of the still

An early view of the Avon Valley at Fox's Wood with the rough temporary roadway to rail level. The riverside cottages on the left are still there.   *Bourne print 1846*

---

[2]*Bristol University Library*

uncompleted masonry. (There is some doubt as to the precise location because the railway is carried on a similar structure between Nos 2 and 3 tunnels - Brunel's Report to the Board[3] does not specify). That was just one of the problems resulting from the very wet winter of 1839. The existence of a retaining wall & arches which support the railway at this point will be unknown to the majority of travellers as the arches can only be seen from the tow path on the opposite bank of the river. The railway is in a very inaccessible area known as Fox's Wood, still very well wooded and with no road access. However, that last statement needs to be qualified because contemporary prints during the very early days of the railway depict a rough track down through the woods which, no doubt, was used for carting material to and from the site. Deer frequent the woods as the author has had the unhappy experience of seeing two animals beside the line, one injured and the other dead.

At a point near mile post 115¼ the river veers away from the railway and the railway enters into a deep cutting wherein were two short tunnels of 53 and 37 yards, both of which were opened out towards the end of the 19th Century. Adjacent to mile post 115¼ there was situated Fox's Wood signal box, to which there was no road access, and which was supervised by the Keynsham Station Master. The author can well remember Mr Bartrum getting on his bike and cycling down the trackside pathway to pay his required daily visit to the box, long before the advent of High Speed Trains. The first box on the site was replaced in July 1922 and its replacement was closed in November 1960 when the semaphore signals were converted to automatic intermediate block colour light signals (IBS).

The necessity for a signal box in such an inaccessible position arose because of a quarry connection. In fact, the quarry was there before the railway and it belonged to the well known

A Western class Diesel Hydraulic in Fox's Wood. The supporting arches prevent the railway from slipping into the river below.   *Author*

---

[3]*PRO Rail 250/82*

A 28xx on a once familiar up mixed goods in Fox's Wood cutting on 1st June 1963. On the left can be seen the disused quarry with blocks of stone still lying around. *Author*

Drs Francis Ker Fox and Charles Joseph Fox of Brislington House (hence Fox's Wood). The quarry mouth is at river level and stone was brought up to rail level by means of an incline plane, shown on the Keynsham tithe map as occupying 15 perches. It would appear from the adjacent Brislington tithe map that the tramroad continued in the direction of Brislington House and the Bristol to Bath turnpike. Strange to relate, whilst the incline plane is shown on the tithe map, the quarry is not, the area concerned being designated withy beds. Brunel made use of that quarry and he got into trouble with the Drs Fox. In order to get the stone up from the river bank to rail level a cable and drum was used. The drum was inadequate to cope with the loads being brought up and, in consequence, became defective. The good doctors required compensation for the damage and threatened to take the Opinion of Learned Counsel. The GWR solicitors, Messrs Osborne Ward and Sons considered that it would be very difficult to assess compensation and persuaded Brunel to go personally to Brislington House and negotiate. Between 16th and 27th December 1839 there were five items of account which cost Brunel and the GWR £1 11s 8d, (£1-58) payable to Osborne Ward and Sons.[4] Not all the stone was taken out by rail, some went by river, including that for the bridge over the Avon at the Netham.[5]

The Ordnance Survey map of 1882 shows railway sidings penetrating right into the heart of the quarry, and one can conjecture that at an earlier date the incline plane was replaced

[4]*GWR Account Book No.5 University of Bristol Library*

[5]*PRO Rail 250/82*

by an adhesion worked siding. Some of the sidings at rail level were still in situ until February 1953.[6] Nothing remains at the riverside except a few stone blocks which were left where they lay when quarrying ceased. Likewise, nothing can be seen from the passing train. Pedestrian access to the quarry has been made much easier by public footpath since the opening of the Bristol Ring Road. The wharf area can be seen from the Ring Road crossing of the River Avon, if viewed from the Bristol side of the bridge

Only a short distance from the Fox's Wood signal box, towards Bath, there was another quarry on the opposite, down side of the line, clearly visible from the train. Very little has been discovered about the site. There was no road access and an entry in the Keynsham UDC Rate Book for 1939[7] clearly indicates that it was railway owned. A rail connection was put in during 1902; acquisition of land was authorised by the GWR Act of 1904 and additional sidings were laid during the First World War. It is not known when that, or the other quarry, ceased operating. The workings were certainly not so extensive as the riverside quarry, but like that quarry, blocks of stone can still be seen lying around. Such sidings as remained were lifted during the February 1953 clear up operation.

The next point of interest is the laying of the water troughs, 500 yards long, which extended nearly up to Durley Lane. For those who cannot remember steam traction, some explanation may be required concerning water troughs. Long metal troughs laid between the rails were filled with water and replenished from an adjacent water tower as and when necessary. If the engine driver of an approaching train needed to replenish his tender water tank, his firemen would lower the tender scoop and the speed of the train would force water up into the engine's tender. It was an operation requiring some skill by the fireman in order to lower and raise the scoop

at the right moment. Failure to raise the scoop in time would overfill the tank with the result that passengers in the front coach could have an unexpected shower through any open windows.

In order to provide the troughs, the first requirement was to have a perfectly level track. Although the gradient of 1 in 1320 was slight, some levelling was necessary. Disposal of surplus soil on to the adjacent land would account for that particular area being known to-day as the Humpty Dumps. The water troughs, brought into use on 30th June 1899, were the second on the GWR[8], although the LNWR had already been using troughs for thirty years.[9] Rapid dieselisation of express passenger trains made the troughs obsolete and they were taken out of use in May 1961, and removed by the following August over four years prior to the end of steam on the Western Region at 31st December 1965. Water softening plant, installed during 1905, was also removed.

In early 1898, there was correspondence between the Keynsham Rural District Council (KRDC) and the railway concerning flooding of the road from Lodge Farm to Durley Hill, for which, the railway denied all liability. In reply thereto, the Clerk to the RDC was directed to write to the GWR on 1st March 1898 stating "that the culvert marked 'A' on the plans sent by the Company had undoubtedly been made by the Company when the water course was diverted and that the liability to keep the same cleansed still remained with them."

The water course still exists and, no doubt, the alterations made by the Company were preparatory to the installation of the water troughs. By August 1898 the RDC had given up, it being minuted "It was left to Mr Richmond to cleanse out the arch of the culvert at Lodge Road so as to prevent flooding of the road there."

The Ordnance Survey map of 1882 shows

---

[6]*PRO Rail 282/264*

[7]*Somerset County Record Office* ◦

[8]*The first were at Basildon between Pangbourne and Goring*

[9]*McDermott*

Auto fitted 0–4–2T 1444 on a down enthusiasts' special on the Hams embankment on 20th September 1964. *Author*

County class 4–4–0 picking up water from the Fox's Wood water troughs. The footbridge over the railway is in the background. *GWR Magazine 1910*

Also on the Hams embankment a sad procession en route to a South Wales scrap merchant's yard. There was 30071, a USA 0–6–0T, Bulleid Battle of Britain pacific 34087 *145 Squadron*, Standard 4–6–0 73118 *King Leodegrance* and another Stardard 4–6–0, 73043. At the head was Peak D26. 9th March 1968.

Author

two public footpaths, one from Hicks Gate (on what is now the Hicks Gate roundabout between Keynsham and the Brislington Trading Estate), and one from the Broombill area of Bristol, joining up to cross the railway on the level at the site of the water troughs. The footpath climbed up the side of the cutting, across the meadow and down the other side to the Hanham ferry. These would have been much used, as it was the shortest route via the ferry to the Gloucestershire side of the river by the Chequers Inn for Hanham and Kingswood. Therefore, once the water troughs were installed, it was essential for the railway to provide a footbridge. To-day, the footbridge sees little use other than by joggers and the few others who are prepared to brave all the obstacles that nature and dereliction has put in the way. Nevertheless, being still a recognised footpath, the railway in recent years has been obliged to spend money in putting the bridge into a good state of repair.

With Lodge Farm above, on the up side,

the railway emerges from the long cutting, crosses Durley Lane (it is all Durley Lane now), and then crosses the Keynsham Hams on a $^3/_4$ mile long, 30ft high embankment. Following the arrival of Fry's chocolate factory in the 1920s, the name 'Somerdale' was embedded into the embankment in large concrete blocks. That became a well known landmark, clearly visible to all who travelled on the then main A4 trunk road into Keynsham as they passed by the Crown Inn. It was at that point that the Bristol Churchgoer had trouble with his steed John Bunyan. The construction of the Keynsham by-pass in the 1960s, parallel to the railway, all but obliterated sight of the landmark. In consequence, maintenance ceased and the concrete deteriorated, although traces can still be seen from the by-pass, albeit subject to the enroachment of vegetation.

Out of the cutting at Lodge Farm, over the Keynsham Hams, into another short cutting and we arrive at Keynsham station.

3. Keynsham Station

Keynsham was the only intermediate station between Bristol and Bath when the line first opened on 31st August 1840. (Saltford and Twerton did not open until later in the year: St Anne's Park not until 1898). At the date of the 1841 Census the population of the Parish of Keynsham was 2307, of whom approximately 9% were either in the workhouse or were paupers.

The railway station is placed within a few minutes walk from the High Street, then the centre of the village. It is also on the very edge of the town (as it is to-day), approximately one hundred yards from the River Avon which, until Local Authority reorganisation in 1974, formed the boundary between the Counties of Somerset and Gloucestershire, Keynsham being on the Somerset side. That geographical boundary has resulted in a nil urban development on the Gloucestershire side, the land being designated green belt. On the other hand, particularly since the end of the war in 1945, there has been a continuous build up of the urban area on the Somerset side, so that the current population of the town approximates to 15,500 (excluding Saltford). Geography has dictated that the development has spread further and further away from the High Street and, therefore, further away from the railway station. The extremities of the development are all of two miles from the High Street and the station. (With the abolition of the unloved County of Avon in 1996 the County boundary appertaining up to 1974 has been restored. It will have no effect on the green belt status of the land on the Gloucestershire side.)

The station is immediately adjacent to the A4175 road, which until 1994, provided the only road crossing of the river between Bristol

Keynsham station at the turn of the century with the original narrow short platforms, uncovered footbridge, the original downside building and signal box. The width between the running lines indicates the one time broad gauge track. *Lens of Sutton*

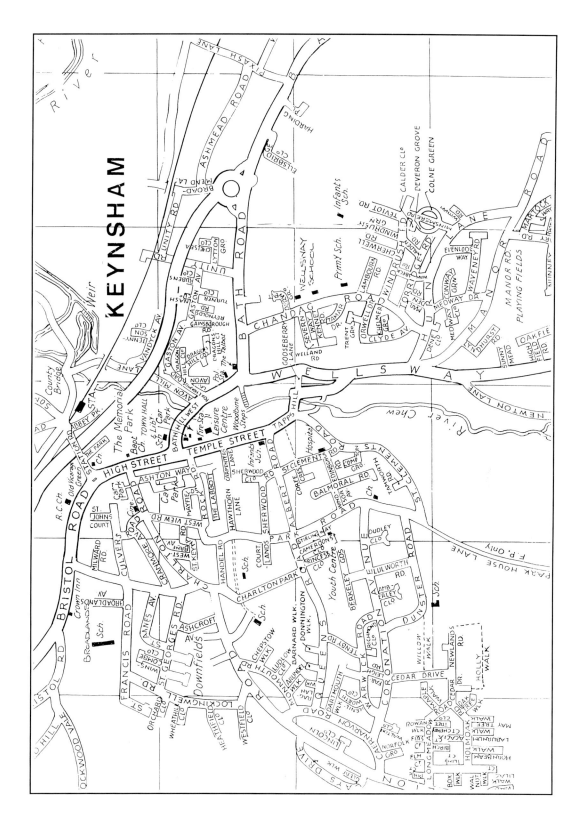

KEYNSHAM

and Bath, therefore, it has always been of strategic importance. Its importance has been significantly diminished by the new river crossing opened in 1994 as part of the Bristol Ring Road scheme.

George Measom in his Official Guide to the Great Western Railway, published in 1861, describes the village of Keynsham thus: "Keynsham consists of a long irregular street, containing several interesting specimens of domestic architecture, one of which is a street front, with a curious bay window, supported on two half-length figures, sculptured in a costume of early date. Some parts of the Church are much admired, particularly the west end of the south aisle with its stairs' turret. The tower was rebuilt in 1612."

There was not much to say about Keynsham in those days.

When constructed in 1840, the main station building and all the facilities were on the up side. George Meason describes the station "as constructed of hammer dressed lias, with Bath stone quoins and dressings and it has an upper story (sic). Bourne in his history dated 1846 states that from Bath towards Bristol the buildings are wholly Gothic. That included the bridgework and the tunnel portals, although he does concede that one of the tunnel fronts was Norman. On the other hand, Vaughan in his Pictorial Record of Great Western Architecture[1] describes the station as Tudor or debased James I. It was a building out of all proportion for a village of little more than two thousand souls. The upper storey provided living accommodation for the Station Master. Although the building is no more, there are still to be seen at Steventon (near Didcot) lineside houses which have an architectural affinity. They are of a contemporary period, constructed by the GWR and designated "Officers houses", being situated at a convenient half way point between Paddington and Bristol.

The principal entrance to the station was on the up side, adjacent to the main building. On the down side platform there was a substantial building of familiar early Brunel

The former Great Western staff houses at Steventon which have an architectural affinity to the Keynsham principal station building. *Author*

---

[1]OPC 1977

The path from Avon Road to the station with the second signal box high up on the embankment.

M.J. Tozer Collection

design which was probably no more than a waiting room. There was also access to the down platform by a footpath from Avon Road which crossed the River Chew by a much photographed wooden bridge. The bridge was washed away in the floods of 1968 and never replaced. The footpath appears on the plan for the Radstock and Keynsham Railway of 1861 (see also page 22) and also on contemporary documents relating to the properties belonging to the then Duke of Buckingham. Therefore, it is quite feasible that the bridge was placed there about the time of the opening of the station in 1840.

In Measom's second edition to his Guide published in 1861, he describes the Keynsham station house: "The floor of a chamber is formed of the tessellated pavement removed from the Roman villa at Newton St Lo (sic). It represents Orpheus playing upon his lyre, around him a circle of beasts - leopards, stags and bulls - supposed to be attracted by the harmony". The first edition of the Guide published in 1852, makes no mention of the pavement. The truth is that the first edition of the Guide was correct, for the pavement was removed into the care of the Bristol Museum (then in Park Street) in 1851! Its location at Keynsham was considered unsuitable. It is now stored, in pieces, in the Bristol City Museum and Art Gallery in Queens Road in a very fragile condition. It has not been assembled since 1930.

However, with great foresight, an engineer, T.E.M. Marsh, made records and illustrations of the villa and the mosaic. The main record of the mosaic is a 1:1 colour tracing made by Marsh in 1837. That too is now very delicate and has deteriorated with age. In order to preserve the record, and in honour of its 150th anniversary, a modern 1:1 copy of the Victorian relic was made in 1987, reduced by Xerox, and hand coloured as Marsh's copy had been. It is now on display in the Bristol City Museum and Art Gallery. (Detailed information supplied by Mrs G. Boyle, the Curator, Prehistoric and Roman Archaeology.)

The made up land to the East of where the

The Roman mosaic which was laid on the floor of a chamber in the station house.

Bristol City Museums and Art Gallery

station house stood, now wooded, and which juts out to overlook the junction of Station Hill with Avon Mill Lane, is shown on the tithe map as the station garden. On that land was constructed the first Keynsham Goods Yard. It consisted of a siding trailing off the up main line, leading to a turntable, off which radiated some short sidings. The yard was shunted by a horse.

Keynsham did not escape the effects of the Railway Mania, a period when all kinds of hare brained schemes appeared on paper, many of which got no further. The mania was at its height in the mid 1840s. In 1845, there was a scheme for a railway from Bristol to Poole, connecting the Bristol Channel with the English Channel. It was proposed that the Bristol Wells and Poole Railway should leave the GWR main line immediately East of Keynsham station and proceed up the Chew Valley and to approach the City of Wells via Ditcheat in the Cheddar Valley.[2]

In 1861 came the Radstock and Keynsham Railway proposal, the main objective being, to obtain an outlet from collieries in the Somerset coalfield, particularly those in the Radstock, Camerton and Paulton areas. Again, the line branched off from the GWR immediately East of Keynsham station, proceeding East of Avon Road, crossing what is now the Dragons Hill estate to a point at the junction of what is now the Wellsway with the Bath Road near to The Pound. The railway was to run along the East side of the Chew Valley, for which purpose Burnett Lane (now Wellsway) was to be diverted to the East as far as Rookhill House. Nothing came of that scheme either.[3]

About 1873, the first signal box was erected at Keynsham, positioned on the down platform. Until that date points and signals were still controlled by hand levers, and trains worked on the time interval system.[4]

Returning to the mid 1840s, Brunel found himself isolated with his broad gauge lines of 7'0¼" because every other major railway had been constructed to the narrow gauge (as it was then known) of 4'8½". Because of the considerable inconvenience caused through the transhipment of goods where broad gauge met narrow gauge notably at Gloucester, Parliament appointed a gauge commission which came out in favour of the narrow gauge. Actually, the Commissioners found much in favour of the broad gauge, but the cost of converting narrow gauge to broad gauge was a non-starter. Tunnels would have required enlargement, embankments, bridges and viaducts widening and stations reconstructed to allow for the additional width of the track. Conversely, the change from broad gauge to narrow gauge only required the provision of an additional rail at 4'8½" laid between the 7'0¼" rails. That became known as the mixed gauge. The Gauge Act of 1846 made 4'8½" the rule and anything else the exception. In practice, the exceptions were almost wholly confined to the construction of broad gauge lines within wholly broad gauge territory.

Having lost the day, the GWR gradually became a mixed gauge line and thus the first narrow, i.e. standard gauge train, arrived at

---

[2]*Bibliotea Somersetensis - Bristol Central Reference Library*

[3]*Somerset County Record Office, Taunton. Ref: Q/Rup277*

[4]*Signalling Record Society*

Paddington in 1861. The Bristol area was well down the list of lines to be treated, so that mixed gauge did not arrive at Bristol (from Trowbridge) until June 1874 and from Chippenham until April 1875. There was then mixed gauge throughout from Paddington to Bristol, and by March 1876 through to Exeter.

Salient points extracted from the February and June 1876 Working Time Tables[5] are as follows:

Of 73 trains (including goods trains) passing through Keynsham every 24 hours on week-days, 37 were broad gauge. It must be remembered that all through trains to the West of England beyond Exeter were of necessity broad gauge. 21 trains each day called at Keynsham, of which, surprisingly eleven were broad gauge. Nine of those were of a local character to and from either Bath, Chippenham or Swindon. The other two were relics of the Parliamentary era, trains to and from Paddington which called at most stations, including Twerton and Saltford which in those days was no more than a hamlet of about 400 souls. They still progressed at little more than the regulation Parliamentary speed. The 2.30pm from Paddington called at Keynsham at 8.52pm, whilst the up train called at 3.40pm, finally wandering into Paddington at 9.55pm, i.e. $6\frac{1}{4}$ hours to cover $113\frac{3}{4}$ miles at an average speed of 18.2 mph.

On Sundays there were fifteen trains which called at Keynsham. There was a train at 8.10am to Weymouth, the return service calling at 8.40pm. There was no regular through train to that popular resort on week-days. (See also Chapter 15 page 120.) The Parliamentary trains took no less than 11hrs 50 mins down and 12hrs 35 mins up between London and Plymouth, and they were the only day time Sunday through services to and from the West of England. Despite the snail's progress, the up train was non-stop between Bristol and Bath.

There were two most interesting trains in the timetable. On Sundays, the 10am broad gauge train from Bristol to Bath did a metamorphosis and returned from Bath to Bristol at 11.15am in the narrow gauge configuration!

On Mondays only, when there was no other traffic about, an empty stone train arrived at Keynsham at the bewitching hour of 2.15am. It returned immediately at 2.20am in the Bristol direction, although not scheduled to arrive there until 5am. It passed the time at Birchwood Quarry which was situated on the downside of the line between the two tunnels at Brislington. Stone quarried during the week was stacked beside the line to await loading on to the early Monday morning train. It was there on 31st March 1876 that a large stone fell on to the line and whilst John Chiddy, a quarryman was trying to remove it he was killed by the two o'clock narrow gauge train from Bath. His grave and memorial are to be found in Christ Church graveyard at Hanham. Hence Memorial Road at Hanham where his cottage may still be seen. "He saved the train but was killed in doing it".[6]

West of Exeter, the lines remained a stronghold of the broad gauge until the epic week-end of 20th-21st May 1892, when during the two day period the whole system was converted from broad gauge to standard gauge. Thus, the last broad gauge passenger trains to pass through Keynsham were the 5pm Paddington to Plymouth, hauled as far as Bristol by the locomotive *Bulkeley* on the evening of Saturday 20th May, and the up mail from Penzance in the small hours of Sunday 21st May, also hauled by the locomotive *Bulkeley*. Thus passed the broad gauge into history. A few broad gauge trains passed through Keynsham after 21st May conveying redundant empty stock to Swindon for breaking up.

The removal of the broad gauge outer rails allowed the up and down lines to be brought closer together. The space saved between the tracks permitted the platform surfaces to be widened by approximately two feet each for the greater convenience and safety of passengers.

In 1887, a refuge siding was constructed on the up side, together with a head shunt where

---

[5] *PRO Rail 937/24 and 25*

[6] *Bristol Times and Mirror 3rd April 1876.*

Up Trains through Keynsham
Weekdays — February 1876

Gauge		Depart Bristol	Call Keynsham	From	To
NG	Goods	12Nt MX		Bristol	Weymouth
BG	Limited Mail	12.40am		Plymouth 7.45pm	Paddington 3.55am
BG	Passenger	12.50		Plymouth 7.45pm	Paddington 4.35am
NG	Goods	1.00 RR		Bristol	Didcot
BG	Loco S-one	2.00	2.15	Bristol	Keynsham
NG	Goods	2.30 MX	2.45–2.55 MX	Bristol	Reading
NG	Goods	3.00 MX		Bristol	Salisbury
NG	Goods	4.30		Bristol	Wells
NG	Passenger	6.20	6.30	Bristol	Salisbury
NG	Goods	6.25		Bristol	Devizes & Oxford
BG	Passenger	7.00		Bristol	Swindon
BG	Passenger	7.30	7.40	Bristol	Bath (not Saltford & Twerton)
BG	Bristol Express	7.50		Bristol	Paddington 10.45am
NG	Goods	7.55		Bristol	Didcot
NG	Passenger	8.50	9.00	Bristol	Swindon
NG	Passenger	10.00		Bristol	Salisbury
BG	Passenger	10.10		Exeter 6am	Paddington 2.30pm
BG	Passenger	11.20	11.30	Bristol	Chippenham
BG	Fast Exeter Express	12.09pm		Plymouth 8.35am	Paddington 2.45pm
BG	Passenger	1.15		Plymouth 6.35am	Paddington 5.15pm
BG	Passenger	1.45	1.55	Bristol	Bath
NG	Passenger	2.10		Bristol	Salisbury

Gauge		Depart Bristol	Call Keynsham	From	To
BG	Western Mail Express	2.45		Plymouth 10.00am	Paddington 6pm
BG	Passenger	3.30	3.40	Plymouth 11.20am	Paddington 9.55pm
NG	Goods	3.40		Bristol	Paddington Goods 1.35pm
NG	Passenger	4.30	4.40	Bristol	Bath (not Saltford)
BG	W of E & London Express Goods	4.45		Plymouth 4.30am	Paddington Goods 12.20am
NG	Passenger	5.20	5.30	Bristol	Westbury
NG	Passenger	6.40	6.50	Bristol	Salisbury (not Saltford & Twerton)
BG	Fast Exeter Express	7.00		Plymouth 2.15pm	Paddington 10.20pm
NG	Goods	8.00		Bristol	Smithfield 2.40am
NG	Express Goods	9.00		Bristol	Birmingham
BG	Passenger	9.15	9.25	Bristol	Bath
BG	Goods	9.30	9.45–9.55	Bristol	Paddington Goods 6am
NG	Passenger	10.15	10.25	Bristol	Bath (not Saltford & Twerton)
BG	Meat & Fish	11.00		Bristol	Paddington Passenger 3.20am

BG   Broad Gauge
NG   Narrow Gauge
MO   Mondays Only
MX   Mondays Excepted
RR   Runs when Required
Authority PRO Rail 937/24

Down Trains through Keynsham
Weekdays — February 1876

Gauge		Depart Bath	Call Keynsham	From	To
NG	Goods	12.40am MX		Salisbury	Bristol
BG	Loco Stone		2.20 MO	Keynsham	Bristol arrive 5am
NG	Goods	2.35 MX		Wells	Bristol
BG	1st Bristol & W of E Express Goods	2.56 MX		Paddington Goods	Bristol
NG	Goods	3.30 MX		Paddington Goods 6.30pm	Bristol
NG	Goods	4.25 MX	5.00–5.10	Weymouth	Bristol
NG	Smithfield & Bristol Express Goods	6.20 MX		Smithfield 12midnight	Bristol
NG	Passenger	7.20	7.35	Bath	Bristol
BG	2nd Bristol Express Goods	7.40 MX		Paddington Goods 1am	Plymouth
BG	Passenger	8.20		Paddington 5.30am	Plymouth 2.58pm
NG	Passenger	8.38	8.55	Salisbury	Bristol
BG	Passenger	9.00	9.25	Bath	Bristol
NG	Express Goods	9.10		Birmingham Hockley	Bristol
BG	Passenger	10.10	10.25	Swindon	Bristol (not Twerton & Saltford)
BG	Fish & Meat empties	11.10 MX	10.25	Paddington Passenger	Bristol
BG	Main Line Express	11.40		Paddington 9am	Plymouth 4.45pm
NG	Passenger	12.06pm		Salisbury	Bristol
NG	Goods	12.20 RR		Didcot	Bristol
NG	Goods	12.40 MX		Reading	Bristol

Gauge		Depart Bath	Call Keynsham	From	To
NG	Passenger	1.00	1.25	Didcot	Bristol
BG	Fast Exeter Express	2.03		Paddington 11.45am	Plymouth 6pm
BG.	Passenger	2.45		Paddington 10.30am	Plymouth 9.40pm
NG	Passenger	3.38		Salisbury	Bristol
BG	Passenger	4.05	4.30	Chippenham	Bristol
BG	Passenger	5.28		Paddington 1.50pm	Exeter 9.55pm
NG	Goods	5.55		Didcot	Bristol
BG	Passenger	6.35	6.55	Bath	Bristol (arrived Bath 6pm from Swindon)
NG	Goods	6.40	7.10–7.15	Oxford &Devizes	Bristol
BG	Main Line Express	7.45		Paddington 5pm	Plymouth 12.10am
NG	Passenger	8.20	8.52	Salisbury	Bristol
NG	Passenger	8.32		Paddington 2.30pm	Bristol
NG	Passenger	9.14	9.35	Salisbury	Bristol
BG	Passenger	10.00	10.15	Bath	Bristol (not Twerton & Saltford)
BG	Passenger	10.50		Bath	Bristol
BG	Goods	11.10 MO		Paddington Goods 2.50pm	Bristol
BG	Passenger	11.40		Paddington 8.10pm	Plymouth 4.40am
BG	Limited Mail	11.57		Paddington 9pm	Plymouth 4.40am

Up Trains through Keynsham
SUNDAYS FEBRUARY 1876

Gauge			Depart Bristol	Call Keynsham	From	To
NG		Goods	12ngt		Bristol	Weymouth
	BG	Limited Mail	12.40am		Plymouth 7.45pm	Paddington 3.55am
	BG	Passenger	12.50		Plymouth 7.45pm	Paddington 4.35am
NG		Goods	2.30	2.45–2.55	Bristol	Reading
NG		Goods	3.00		Bristol	Salisbury
NG		Goods	4.30		Bristol	Wells
NG		Passenger	8.00	8.10	Bristol	Weymouth
	BG	Passenger	10.00	10.10	Bristol	Bath
NG		Passenger	1.00pm	1.10	Bristol	Bath
	BG	Passenger	1.45		Plymouth 6.40am	Paddington 7.15pm
NG		Passenger	3.45	3.57	Bristol	Trowbridge
	BG	Goods	4.05		Bristol	Paddington Goods
NG		Passenger	5.45	5.55	Bristol	Salisbury
	BG	Passenger	6.30	6.42	Plymouth 12.40pm	Paddington 10.50pm (not Saltford & Twerton)
NG		Passenger	9.00	9.10	Bristol	Bath

28

Down Trains through Keynsham
SUNDAYS FEBRUARY 1876

Gauge			Depart Bath	Call Keynsham	From	To
NG		Goods	12.40am		Salisbury	Bristol
NG		Goods	2.35		Wells	Bristol
NG		Goods	4.25	5.00–5.10	Weymouth	Bristol
NG		Goods	6.20		Paddington Goods	Bristol
	BG	Goods	7.40		Paddington Goods	Bristol
NG		Express Goods	8.45		Birmingham Hockley	Bristol
NG		Passenger	10.05	10.28	Salisbury	Bristol
	BG	Passenger	11.15	11.35	Bath	Bristol (NG in June timetable)
NG		Goods	12.25pm		Reading	Bristol
NG		Passenger	2.07	2.22	Trowbridge	Bristol (not Twerton & Saltford)
	BG	Passenger	2.52	3.13	Paddington 10am	Plymouth 9.50pm
NG		Passenger	4.00	4.20	Bath	Bristol
	BG	Passenger	7.15	7.30	Paddington 2.30pm	Bristol (not Twerton & Saltford)
NG		Passenger	8.20	8.40	Weymouth	Bristol
NG		Passenger	9.40	10.00	Bath	Bristol
	BG	Passenger	11.42		Paddington 8.10pm	Plymouth 4.40pm
	BG	Limited Mail	11.57		Paddington 9am	Plymouth 4.40pm

A broad gauge train at Bathampton. *GRW Magazine 1939*

the buffers were up against the parapet of the Bristol side of the Station Road bridge. The Board of Trade Inspector gave approval for the siding to be brought into use on 15th November 1887.[7] It was taken out of use at the end of 1930 when the station platforms were extended in connection with the replacement of the bridge. (See chapter 7). It is difficult now to even appreciate that there was once a third line of track extending out towards the Hams embankment.

Towards the end of Victoria's reign agitation built up for provision of an alternative line between Bristol and London, as there was dissatisfaction with the service provided by the GWR. That resulted in the promotion of the Bristol London and Southern Counties Railway which would have finished up at Waterloo. On 18th February 1903, the Keynsham Parish Council in Meeting agreed to congratulate Messrs Burchell, the Parliamentary Agents, wishing them success and asking for a station at Keynsham to be provided at a convenient spot. A month later, the Parish Council agreed

to sign a petition in favour of the undertaking. The Bill was thrown out of Parliament for the simple reason that those who wanted the railway, including the Keynsham Parish Council, were not prepared to back it with that essential ingredient - money.

In 1907 the GWR board authorised major improvements to the station amenities and facilities in order to better cater for a general increase in traffic. There were dramatic changes at the passenger station.

1. A solid stone built edifice was constructed on the down side set back from the platform face. To do that it was necessary to cut back into the bank behind the platform and to construct a stone retaining wall which is there to this day. The station area being at one time within the domain of the former Keynsham Abbey (Dissolved by King Henry VIII in 1539), it comes as no surprise to learn that during the excavations two stone coffins were unearthed, each complete with a skeleton.

The new downside building included the booking office, waiting room, the station

[7]*PRO MT6/446/9*

This photograph can be dated with some precision as c1909. The footbridge received a roof during the 1908 improvements. The signal box still on the platform was replaced by one on the embankment about 1910. The departing train has just passed under the original Brunel bridge carrying Station Road over the railway: Measom's most handsome bridge on the line. *Lens of Sutton*

master's office, ladies and gentlemen's toilets. Just inside the waiting room door, on the left was the booking office window, and on the opposite wall was the fireplace, complete with a coal fire during the winter months. The booking office also had a door leading on to the platform.

2. The short platforms were extended by 80ft to the maximum length available, being restricted by the parapets on the bridge over the River Chew at the East end, and the parapets of the original bridge under Station Road at the West end. Even so, the up side became only 383ft in length whilst the down side was 430ft, sufficient for no more than six or seven of the short non corridor coaches of the day. The presence of a loading dock on the up side accounts for the shorter platform on that side.

3. With the transference of the amenities to the down side, it was considered necessary to provide another access on that side. There was already a footpath from Avon Road to the station with just a few steps down to the platform, but situated at the far East end of the station. The footpath continued behind the station to Station Road and it was half way along that path that a new entrance was constructed with two flights of ugly concrete steps down to platform level.

4. The footbridge connecting the two platforms was provided with a roof. After completion of all the works under the 1907 scheme the original up side building was used for little more than a parcels office and a left luggage facility.

At the bottom of the footbridge on the up side there was a small stone cabin which did duty as a porters' room, but that was there prior to the alterations just described.

On the goods side, traffic was increasing to such an extent that an additional checker was taken on in 1908. It could not have been easy to deal with the extra traffic with only two short sidings radiating off a turntable and shunted by a horse. Hence the need for additional facilities. The centre of activity was the construction of a new goods shed on the

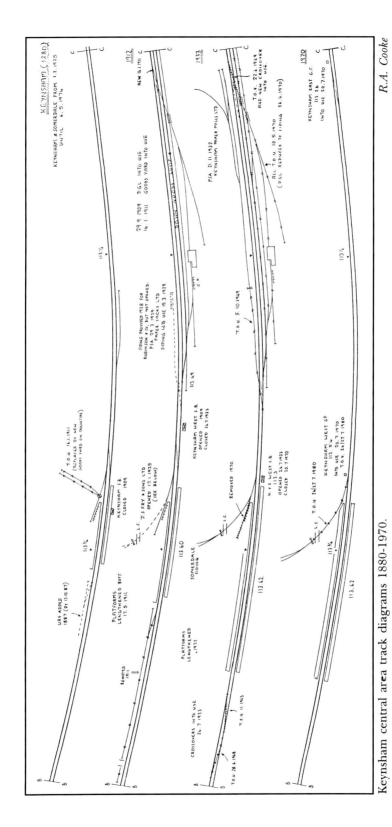

Keynsham central area track diagrams 1880-1970.

R.A. Cooke

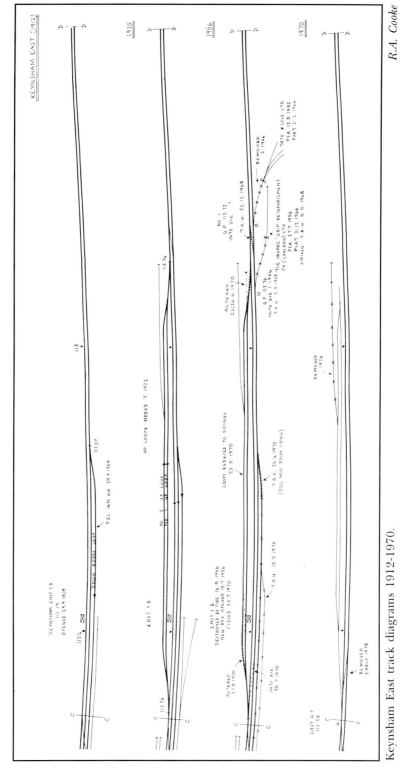

KEYNSHAM EAST (1912)

R.A. Cooke

Keynsham East track diagrams 1912-1970.

33

down side with an entrance off Avon Road. Also provided was a much needed down goods loop with a capacity for 102 wagons, ancillary sidings and cattle pens. The new goods yard was opened for business on 16th January 1911 and the horse became redundant. The following trains were rostered to deal with the Keynsham traffic:

Down Trains

8.50am Hallatrow	to Bristol	calling	1.50pm to 2.27pm
6.15am Didcot	to Bristol		5.35pm to 6.25pm
8.30am Didcot	to Bristol		not specified
5.10pm Swindon	to Plymouth Laira		To put off cattle traffic as required.

The time allowed to get from Hallatrow, via Camerton, and from Didcot to Keynsham should be noted. No doubt, those pick up goods called at, and leisurely shunted, at every wayside station on the way.

Up Trains

8.40am Bristol	to Didcot	calling	8.55am to 9.47am
1.50pm Bristol	to Chippenham (SX)		2.2pm to 2.37pm
4.38pm Bristol	to Chippenham (SO)		4.50pm to 5.15pm
6.25pm Bristol	to Warminster		6.37pm to 6.48pm

The provision of the new goods yard necessitated an alteration to the signalling arrangements. Technology of the day dictated that the pointwork at the Bath end of the new down loop was too far away to be worked from the then existing signal box on the down station platform. Therefore, an additional box was constructed , known as Keynsham East, situated more or less halfway between Broadmead Lane and Pixash Lane, on the up side of the line, adjacent to MP 113¼. It was opened on 29th September 1909, destroyed by fire on 15th May 1956 and replaced on 17th July 1956.

The signal box of 1873 on the down platform was in the way of redevelopment, so it was replaced by a new structure placed on the side of the embankment half way between the station and Avon Road.

Ignoring the capital charges, the day to day running costs for the entire scheme were properly costed out, showing that there would be a net saving of £7.4.0d (£7-20) per annum. Balanced against the additional manpower required, the principal saving arose from the elimination of the horse shunting at 45/- (£2-25) per week, or £169 per annum.[8]

For the period under review, the staffing arrangements were:

1907	Station Master	2 salaried	9 wages	
1908			10 wages	Extra checker, due to increased traffic.
1911		3 salaried	11 wages	Opening of the new goods depot.

[8]*PRO Rail 253/531*

The total included passenger, goods, and signalmen. No extra signalmen were employed. East box was only open for one shift per day and the man was obtained by switching out Twerton and Saltford boxes for a part of one shift each.

The growth of traffic at Keynsham, both passenger and goods, necessitated various changes to the track layout during the period 1930-33. As a result, a new signal box (the third) was constructed just off the end of the down platform. It was built by the well known local firm of Edward Wiggins & Son for a cost of £542. The fitting out estimated cost added £233.[9] It was opened on 24th July 1933 and the signal box of 1909 on the embankment was closed and demolished, but the foundations remain to this day. All three signal boxes were within a hundred yards of each other.

There was further track widening in 1932 when two loop lines were installed on the up side, with a capacity for 63 wagons each, adjacent to the Keynsham East signal box, and that involved a further widening of the Broadmead Lane bridge.

All the Brunel bridges between Bristol and Bath were constructed in the Gothic style (that is with a pointed apex), most of which survive to this day. The later additions to the Unity Road and Broadmead Lane bridges have curved arches. Therefore, a visual inspection from road level shows that there are two separate bridges, side by side at Unity Road, and three bridges, side by side, at Broadmead Lane, with the original Gothic one in the middle. That those bridges are inadequate in width and height for to-day's road traffic is another matter. Heavy Goods Vehicles (HGVs) are faced with the narrow Pixash Lane hump bridge and the narrow and inadequate Stidham Lane in order to gain access to the Broadmead Lane Industrial Estate on the bank of the River Avon.

---

[9]*PRO Rail 250/181*

4. The Country Station

Keynsham, the country station was typical of its kind in its day. The Station Master was lord of all he surveyed. Not only was he responsible for the conduct of his station, but also for the goods yard and all the signal boxes within his domain. He was a person of some status within his local community and, as such, he was expected to promote the railway to the tradespeople and the local farmers. (The farmers brought considerable business to the railway). He was also the railway's representative when dealing with organisations such as the local Council. Perhaps, his most important responsibility was to ensure that all his staff gave strict adherence to the Rules and Regulations which were (and still are) voluminous.

Today, the typical country station is a bare unstaffed platform, perhaps with a utility type bus shelter affording the only refuge from the hostile elements. Happily, the restored railways have come to the rescue with some delightful examples of what used to be, sometimes even with a coal fire in the waiting room. Very often the original station buildings survived and they have been refurbished to a very high standard. Nostalgia has also been engendered by the TV Companies who, thereby, have enriched the coffers of the said railways.

In 1907 the railway produced a handbook entitled "Towns and Villages served by the GWR". It well illustrates the fierce competition that existed between the railways themselves for traffic. The preamble said "This book is intended to be a guide for the Company's staff when dispatching

GOODS AND PARCELS

for places served by the Company's stations: and *in the absence of specific orders from senders*; and to especially indicate those places which

although having stations on other Company's lines can be conveniently served by GWR Stations, for instance:

FISHPONDS - with a station on the Midland Railway - but is within the GWR Company's Lawrence Hill free cartage area."

For Keynsham and other local areas the entries were as follows:

KEYNSHAM
Distance from station $^{1}/_{4}$ mile
GWR agent
Goods and parcels collected and delivered.
(Not a free service if the work carried out by an agent).

SALTFORD
Goods - Keynsham $2^{1}/_{2}$ miles or Bath 5 miles
No free delivery or collection
Parcels free delivery or collection by GWR porter within half mile of the station.

BITTON
Traffic to Keynsham - 2 miles.
No delivery or collection.

CHEWTON KEYNSHAM
and COMPTON DANDO.
Goods and parcels to Keynsham.
No delivery or collection.

Certainly Bitton was not conveniently served by the GWR at Keynsham when there was a Midland Railway station on the doorstep.

The Keynsham agent was Charles Stokes and the first reference to him appeared in Wright's Bristol Directory for 1907. Entries in the Directory for 1909 and 1921 were as follows:

1909	Stokes	Charles	Grocer, baker and coal merchant
			Carting Agent for the GWR High Street
1921	Stokes	Charles C. & Sons	Corn merchants and carting agent for the GWR 38 High Street and Beech House. Telephone 9

The pilot signing for a consignment of Fry's cocoa destined for India at Somerdale on the occasion of the initial trial flight. 13th September 1932   *Cadbury Ltd*

No record has been uncovered as to when Stokes was appointed the carting agent for Keynsham, neither is there any indication of the arrangements appertaining prior to his appointment. What is known is that the railway dispensed with his services in 1930 and took over the work themselves.

Parcels

Post 1930, Keynsham had its own delivery/collection van and driver, based on the passenger station. Each week-day, other than Saturday, the van was loaded with the mountain of parcels for delivery which had been brought out from Bristol on one of the early morning passenger trains. There would also have been other consignments which had accumulated from other services during the previous day. The procedure was reversed at the end of the day when the van returned with parcels for despatch to a multiplicity of destinations, mostly via Bristol.

It was probably in 1964 or 1965, as part of the general run down of the station, that the parcels work was merged with that at Bristol Temple Meads. It was certainly an exercise in economics which avoided double handling at Keynsham, together with the extra hazards of damage or loss in transit.

Perhaps the service provided by the railway was not all that it could have been, for the following paragraph appeared in the Bristol Divisional Manager's report to Paddington for 1932:[1]

"On Tuesday, 13th September, Messrs J.S. Fry & Sons inaugurated an air service from Somerdale for urgent requirements. The aeroplane, loaned from the Bristol Airport at Whitchurch, was utilised for the initial flight and Lord Apsley officiated on behalf of the Air Ministry. 42 first class passengers travelled down by train from

[1]PRO Rail 253/552

London to Keynsham and Somerdale to attend the ceremony. The innovation is in the nature of an experiment and only infrequent trips are made at present."

The Post Office

Probably into the 1960s, the postman met specified trains at Keynsham, delivering mail bags into the custody of the guard and, at the same time, receiving bags from him. The GPO also maintained a telephone call box on the down platform, but that was removed during the early 1960s due to lack of custom.

Milk

Milk traffic was an important source of passenger traffic revenue at Keynsham. For 1910, a total of 4765 churns were despatched by passenger train, earning £271 16s 5d (£271-82) for the station. In reality, that amounted to no more than 13 churns each day, including Sundays. There was a considerable fluctuation in the level of the traffic, 1907 was a nadir with only 1,390 churns despatched, whereas 1914 was a peak with 6,636. Overall, milk was an important source of revenue for the railway. Within the Bristol Division, which stretched right down to Weymouth, 1914 was a peak year with 1,733,720 churns despatched, earning £111,259.1.11d, a considerable sum of money in those days. Multiply those figures up for the country as a whole and they become astronomical. Even such an unlikely station as Lawrence Hill despatched its daily quota. Churns were of 17 or 10 gallon capacity and the milk weighed 10.31lbs per gallon, excluding the weight of the churns.

The Divisional Manager at Bristol reported in 1926 the loss of milk traffic to road competition by tanker. The railway responded in kind when in October 1927 United Dairies introduced 3,000 gallon rail tankers.

To take one example, the Co-operative established a depot adjacent to Puxton and Worle station on the main line to the West of England. The full tanks were collected by an up service, which in 1953 was the 5.55pm milk train from Wellington (Som) and conveyed to a receiving depot at West Ealing. That train

ran via Badminton and so did not pass through Keynsham. However, the return empties passed through at 5.35pm on weekdays, the six or seven tanks being positioned between the engine and the passenger coaches on the 4.7pm from Swindon.

The last recorded date for milk traffic at Keynsham was 1932, Sadly, the railway is now out of the milk business altogether.

Racehorses

Keynsham station was in the racehorse business because a stud was maintained at Lodge Farm. Horses would have been loaded and unloaded at the loading dock on the up side at the Bath end of the platform. Horseboxes were quite small vehicles with a compartment adjacent to the horse for the benefit of the groom. Horseboxes either travelled by passenger train or as a special horse box train. Mr A.W. Pillers was the manager of the Keynsham stud according to Kelly's directory for 1906 and he resided at Buckingham Lodge in Station Road.[2] The stud groom was a Mr Charles Newman. In 1933 there was a significant increase in horse traffic: 18 were despatched and 18 received - in all probability the same 18 being returned home. The increase in traffic was attributed to a new trainer, named as a Mr Davis.

In 1933, the Shepton Mallet Journal reported as follows:

"More racehorses are carried annually by the GWR than any other railway company. This year it is expected between 12,000 and 14,000 will be conveyed to and from meetings throughout the country and the various training centres on the system. Rail transport for these sensitive creatures has proved to be the least tiring form of transport and so little are they affected by the journey that they are fit to race shortly after detraining."

Sunday School Outings

A source of revenue for all railways until quite recent years was the Sunday School outing. Until late into the 19th Century, it was a case of tea in the Church Hall, followed by games in a local field by courtesy of the owner. Once

---

[2]*Buckingham Lodge is now known as 1 Abbey Park*

Sunday School outing to Weston-super-Mare in the penultimate year. 19th June 1961. *Author*

the Schools started to venture outside Keynsham the popular destination became Weston-super-Mare. There is evidence that the Anglicans were going there in the early 1880s, and by 1886 the Baptists were following suit: a Minute dated 21st June of that year resolved "to take the children to Weston-super-Mare for their treat and that 10/- (50p) be spent on toys etc." Travel in those days over such a comparatively long distance could only be by train.

The Bristol Divisional Superintendent, in his report for 1909 stated that 140 Baptists from Keynsham went to Weston-super-Mare on 7th July, and that nine days later, on 16th July, another 500 travelled, undoubtedly from the Parish Church. To give some idea of the extent of the traffic, in 1920 he reported that there were no fewer than 110 special Sunday School trains to Weston-super-Mare, conveying 79,000 passengers.

During the inter-war years some of the Keynsham Sunday Schools went to Weston by char-a-banc. Up to the immediate post war years the schools went their own independent ways and arranged their own midweek dates, much to the inconvenience of the local day schools. The Vicar tried to get a common agreed date back in 1906 between the five schools but failed. (Anglicans, Baptists, and the Methodists at Bethesda, Victoria and Zion). A new post war Combined Sunday Schools Committee achieved success in 1950, although, unfortunately, it proved to be a very wet day.[3]

A newspaper report in 1954 stated that the Keynsham and Saltford day schools closed on Friday, 22nd June, on the occasion of the annual outing of Sunday Schools, when four hundred Church of England, Zion and Victoria Methodist went to Weston-super-Mare by train. Bethesda Methodists and the Baptists made their own way to Weston by coach. The following year, the Baptists, at least, joined the chartered train and found it cheaper than the

[3]*The History of Keynsham Baptist Church - Russell Leitch (1985)*

coaches. The rapid growth of the town with the consequent opening of new day schools found the head teachers less co-operative for a general close down, so 1962 proved to be the last year for combined weekday outings.

THE GOODS YARD

Keynsham, like many country stations, not only had a goods yard, but also a goods shed. That at Keynsham was of a standard GWR design, constructed in red brick with one through line adjacent to a loading platform. The loading platform also incorporated the goods office.

Being open at each end, the platform could be a cold and draughty place to work, especially as one end faced due east. The building, erected in 1911, still stands, but was defaced in 1990 by the closing off of the eastern opening with concrete blocks.

The Railway Clearing House Handbook of Stations, dated 1929, included the following entry:

Keynsham and Somerdale   G P F L H C
Crane power 6T 0Cwt
G   Goods traffic
P   Passenger, Parcels and Miscellaneous
     Traffic

Panoramic view of the line looking towards Bath with the goods yard in the centre and the paper mill siding to the left.
Courtesy Mrs A. Frere

F	Furniture Vans, Carriages, Motor Cars, Portable Engines, Machines on Wheels
L	Live Stock
H	Horse Boxes and Private Cattle Vans
C	Carriages, Motor Cars by Passenger and Parcel Trains Somerdale Siding (Fry J.S.& Sons)

The list was comprehensive but there was no mention of a weighbridge.

At that date (1929), the railway had still to feel the effects of a slowly growing competition from the infant road transport industry. Household removals were common place, the goods and chattels being packed into 'B' type containers and conveyed to and from the local goods station on flatbed lorries. Less common, but more spectacular, by virtue of the organisation involved, was the removal of a farm, animals included. If necessary, the special train would be sidelined en route to permit the milking of the cows. A passenger coach was attached to the train for the convenience of the farmer, his family and the farm hands.

Cartage

Stokes was the agent for carting until the railway dispensed with his services in 1930 and took over the job themselves. The changeover was part of an ongoing exercise being carried out at that period. The advantage was said to be that it speeded up operations considerably, as the railway had an incentive to unload wagons and clear the yard as quickly as possible, thus giving a better service. Delays, which incurred demurrage charges on standing wagons, were unpopular with both farmers and traders.

The largest regular customers requiring cartage were:

Polysulphin and
Gould Thomas

Polysulphin was a manufacturer of industrial soaps and its premises were situated on the river bank at the far end of Broadmead Lane. Most of the raw material came in by rail, but from quite early days the finished products went out by road using ex-Army World War I vehicles. Closely associated with the firm in its later days was Ivo Peters of Somerset and Dorset Railway fame.

Gould Thomas traded as Drysalters, in the manufacture of vegetable dyes from dyewoods imported from various parts of the world. Later, they incorporated the making of Glauber Salts and Ammonium Chloride, for which purposes carboys of acid were received by rail. The firm operated from the Logwood Mill (or Albert Mill) situated at the bottom of Dapps Hill (Note: shown as Tapps Hill in error on official map p19).

By the turn of the Century Keynsham was a slowly expanding community, so that materials for house building would have to come in by rail and be carted to site. During the inter war years there was considerable incoming traffic associated with the construction of the Somerdale chocolate factory and also the building of employee housing in the Chandos Road area. In the early 1930s the other major construction work was the Keynsham Paper Mill. As late as the early post war years much of the material for the construction of Newton Park College at nearby Corston was routed through Keynsham Goods.

Livestock

Until more recent times, the railway had a virtual monopoly in the conveyance of livestock. The author can remember up to the end of the 1950s cattle and sheep being driven from the goods yard along Avon Road (before it was bisected by the by-pass), out into Bath Hill East and then either along Bath Road or up the Wellsway. Keynsham Cattle Market, adjacent to the Talbot Hotel, Bath Road, provided a quota of business in the opposite direction, animals being driven on the hoof from the market to the goods yard.

The railway treated their livestock traffic very seriously. There is a report of Mr Frederick Pither of Chewton Keynsham, who retired from the GWR in 1913 at the age of 73, with 56 years service. At the date of his retirement he was the District Cattle Inspector.

One of the less salubrious jobs in the yard was the cleaning out of the cattle pens and cattle wagons - a job that is no longer necessary because the railway no longer possesses such a thing as a cattle wagon!

Agricultural Shows

Agricultural Shows brought good business to

the railway and there were far more locations than there are to-day. Except for purely local traffic, all animals and equipment were brought in by rail and taken away again after the show. The Divisional Superintendent recorded three such shows in 1914 where traffic was provided for Keynsham:

15th May	The return special, en route to Salisbury, from the Somerset County Show held at Weston-super-Mare, had three vans for Keynsham.
24th June	was the occasion of the Wilts County Show at Chippenham, when the return special put off one van with one cow at Keynsham
3rd July	The Royal Agricultural Show was held at Shrewsbury and there were three vans on the return special for Keynsham.

Agricultural Show

Agricultural Show traffic recommenced after the war, for on 20th April 1926 Keynsham dispatched four trucks to Devizes Fair, containing eight cattle and 107 sheep.

Agricultural Shows also attracted passenger traffic with cheap excursion fares available from a wide catchment area. Sometimes there were special trains laid on, as for the Royal Agricultural Show at Shrewsbury on 3rd July 1914. On that occasion there was a train starting from Weymouth at 5.10am, which called to pick up at Keynsham at 8.8am. The weary excursionists, having trudged around the show ground all day, finally made it back to Keynsham at 10.24pm, but it was not until 1.25am next morning that the train finally came to a stand at Weymouth-if it was on time!

The Coal Yard

Every country station had its coal yard. The coal was delivered by rail and laboriously shovelled out of the trucks into the coal merchant's rented allotted space in the yard. Normally, the merchant would have several bunkers into which coal would be stored according to grade. The coal was weighed into 1cwt sacks on a portable weighing machine and hawked around Keynsham and surrounding villages. Saltford had its own coal

yard until 1959 and Bitton until 1965. The whole operation was subject to spot checks (and still is) by the Local Authority's Weights and Measures Department. That did not stop the more unscrupulous merchants from well watering the coal, especially during a period of dry weather. Many a ton of water has been sold that way.

Some coal merchants had their own private owner coal wagons, Charles Stokes of Keynsham being one of them. His wagon, No 1 was illustrated in the Keynsham Parish Council's Official Guide for 1927. Whether he had any more wagons can only be speculative, but it was a good advertising ploy. The advertisement also included that he was

A purveyor of poultry and game foods
A purveyor of Carter's seeds for Farm and Garden
Crushing, grinding and chaff cutting done on the premises.

Stokes coal wagon No 1.
Keynsham Parish Council Guide 1927

The Keynsham Urban District Council's Rate Book for 1939 records that in addition to C.C. Stokes & Sons Ltd, there were two other coal merchants in the yard, i.e. Ernest White and Sydney William White. Post war, merchants who can be remembered at Keynsham were Lowell Baldwin and Renwick Wilton and Dobson, both firms with widespread other business interests.

Central heating, together with modern gas and electric fires has just about killed off the domestic coal trade. The last merchant to operate from the yard was David Hathaway who moved out in 1989, concentrating his activities on his depot at Clutton. His bulk supplies are delivered by road to the one time station yard at Clutton. The station on the Bristol to Frome line closed for both passenger and goods in 1963.

Zoneing

A major reorganisation of goods depots took place after World War II and affected Keynsham in 1950. Effectively, Keynsham thereafter dealt only with full wagon load and private siding traffic. All small consignments were collected, or delivered, by railhead road transport based on the Bristol Temple Meads Goods Department. The benefits included avoidance of transhipment delays, overnight transit between railheads leading to next day deliveries and, on occasion, the make up by the railhead of full wagon loads for one destination.

Upon implementation of the new arrangements, the Keynsham clerical staff were redeployed elsewhere.

The inevitable result of that decision was that by the end of the decade there were no up trains calling at Keynsham Goods to either pick up or detach traffic. In the down direction the Chippenham Goods called as follows:

	Chippenham depart	Called Keynsham
SO	4.0pm	5.17 - 6.10pm
FSX	4.30	5.42 - 5.58
FO	6.15	7.2 - 7.27

There was also a 10.30pm from Weymouth to Bristol East Depot on Saturday nights which called at Keynsham in the early hours of Sunday morning to detach traffic between 5.19 and 5.35. Very strange.

Communication with the outside world was maintained by No 10 transfer from East Depot, arriving shortly after six in the morning, returning to Bristol around mid-day, sometimes combined double-headed with the No 10 Fry's transfer.

Incoming traffic included coal for the paper mill and steel for the Square Grip Reinforcement Co's siding (see chapter 11). There was also household coal for the merchants who had rented accommodation in the yard. On an as required basis there was a delivery of household coal to the station yard at Saltford until the yard closed in 1959. The main consist of the train on its return journey to Bristol would be the empties accumulated during the morning.

Carting Vehicles

Until the date of zoning there was one ancient flat bed lorry based on Keynsham, described as a museum piece and possibly the one originally allocated back in 1930. The driver was one Ern' Cowdery. The vehicle was restricted to light duties in and around Keynsham. For country work recourse was made to Bristol-based lorries. On a lighter note, during the period we are now considering, there was the occasional consignment to a certain establishment at Corston. The carter had strict instructions to deliver the consignment into the personal hands of the Sister Superior (or whatever she was called). It is understood that the bottles contained something stronger than water.

Closure

Post World War II, the transfer of general merchandise traffic from rail to road is a too familiar topic to require any comment here. Sufficient to say, the natural progress of decline was hastened by the Beeching Axe which rapidly chopped down those establishments said to be unprofitable. Keynsham Goods closed on 29th November 1965. At the date of closure, the Chief Goods Clerk was Mr Len Watts who had transferred over from the booking office when the previous occupant of the post, Mr Walter Pope retired in September 1956. Mr Watts arrived at Keynsham from Castle Cary in 1929 and retired when the yard closed. Mr Pope was a well known Methodist local preacher in his day: and a career railwayman, joining at Warminster in 1913. He became Chief Goods Clerk at Keynsham in 1945

The last known use of the yard as a railway yard was on Sunday 10th May 1970 When the girders for the new Bath Hill bridge were collected from the yard and transported the short distance along Avon Mill Lane. But NO! The girders were first taken to the Broadmead roundabout so they could be correctly placed to be craned into position. Whether the girders were actually brought to Keynsham by rail is not known, but at that date the rails were still in situ in the yard.

Since closure, the goods yard has been occupied by a variety of tenants who have both come and gone. Currently, the yard has been largely taken over by stone specialists Drings of Bath who have recently completed a million pound plus expansion project. They aim to become one of the largest and most modern stonemasons in the country. At the far end David Hathaway, the coal merchant, having transferred his household coal depot to Clutton, now uses his portion of the yard as a base for his haulage business.

Statistics

The traffic statistics (See Appendix D) show that the Goods Department at Keynsham was very busy indeed. Physically, much of the traffic went directly into, or out of the private sidings, but the paperwork had to be dealt with in the Goods Department office. As we will see later, the start up of the Somerdale plant and the despatch of its products by rail caused chaos, the office being overwhelmed with paper.

Overall, for the quarter century 1925-49, for which detailed statistics are available, 1,874,551 tons of merchandise passed through the books at Keynsham Goods, of which almost half a million tons was coal. A large proportion of the coal went direct into the Somerdale plant or the Paper Mill sidings.

5. Train Services

In the 19th Century, Keynsham had the sort of country station now so lovingly and nostalgically recreated for us by preservation societies up and down the country, complete with a coal fire in the waiting room when the weather requires it. Keynsham was such a station, where stopping trains called as they made their leisurely way towards Swindon or to the Westbury line, although some got no further than Saltford or Bath.

The picture of the railways' comfortable monopoly of public transport was rudely shattered at the end of the 19th Century by the arrival of the electric tramway, followed not so long afterwards by the omnibus. The Great Western was alarmed and the immediate answer was the rail motor car. Between 1903 and 1908, 99 rail motor cars were constructed, consisting of a passenger coach with an integral small steam locomotive. The outfit could be driven from either end, but the fireman was always on the footplate.

Those rail motor cars rapidly fell out of favour with the authorities in areas where they generated more traffic than they were able to cope with, ie there was overcrowding. A few of the cars survived on the less important branch lines until the 1930s. In their place came auto fitted steam locomotives capable of working push pull with up to four auto coaches sandwich fashion. Like their predecessors, they could be driven from either end, with the fireman being always on the footplate. Although long vanished from Keynsham, auto trains survived working into Bath right up to the time of dieselisation in 1959. A few auto fitted locomotives and trailers survive to this day in preservation.

The services worked by the rail motor cars or by the more conventional autos were both distinguished in the timetable by the letter 'm'

A steam rail motor car at Twerton station on a service from Bristol. Undated.   *Author's collection*

2–4–0 481 of 1869 prior to its renewal in 1889 seen at Keynsham on mixed gauge track.

M.J. Tozer collection

at the head of the appropriate column, the footnote also indicating that it was one class only. The 1910 timetable shows on week-days seven such services calling at Keynsham, one to Chippenham, one to Trowbridge, one to Saltford and four to Bath. In the reverse direction there were eight trains, one each from Chippenham, Frome and Trowbridge one starting at Keynsham, and four from Bath. The first three trains in the morning were all worked by rail motor cars or auto fitted services from Keynsham into Bristol, at 6.30 (from Bath), 7.22 (from Chippenham) and 8.2 (from Frome). There were also four up and three down services so worked on Sundays.

At a meeting held on 5th March 1923[1] it was agreed that the 0-6-0 allocated for the 11.15am from Trowbridge to Bath should be changed to a 2-4-0 Barnum. The remainder of that roster was the 1.40pm from Bath to Bristol and the 5.15pm back to Trowbridge. The train would have sat in the middle road at Bath for

about two hours, and again at Bristol for another three hours. That illustrates the inefficient utilisation of rolling stock, a common enough practice right down to the days of dieselisation. It is also of interest to note that the sobriquet 'Barnum' was recognised in official circles.

The use of 0-6-0s and small tender engines, such as Barnums, on local passenger services was drastically cut back at the end of the 1920s when Swindon constructed 100 new 2-6-2Ts of the 4575 class, of which, approximately half were allocated to the Bristol Division.

During the inter war years, the Minute Books of the Keynsham Parish Council make reference to correspondence with the railway on topics still familiar to-day, such as inconvenient gaps in the service. In 1923 the Council complained to the railway that there was no train from Bath to Bristol calling at Keynsham between 5.5pm and 6.40pm. They received the same sort of answer as we get to-

---

[1]*PRO Rail 253/543*

day, "...... it had been carefully considered, but it was not possible owing to......". Nevertheless, two months later the Minutes reported that an extra train had been put on.

In a Minute dated 12th November 1923, there was a complaint about overcrowding on the 12.40pm from Temple Meads on Saturdays.

On 11th January 1926 it was Minuted "The morning trains to Bristol at 7.53 and 8.40 are unsuitable timings, can they be altered to 8 o'clock and 8.30?

Things have not changed much over the years, except that the media will now make headline news out of it.

To be fair the Parish Council also complained to the Bus Company, an example being about the bus service, or rather lack of it on Sunday evenings when all the buses passed through Keynsham full. There was also an attempt to get the return halves of bus and rail tickets interchangeable, but the Bus Company would not agree because their fares were cheaper than rail.

In 1934 the GWR introduced streamlined AEC internal combustion rail cars with internal fittings up to the best passenger standards of the day. A number of those railcars worked in the Bristol area, including one of the twin sets, the true forerunner of the DMUs. Right from the start on 17th February 1936 single cars were working the 8 o'clock from Bristol to Weymouth. By the 1950s, it was the 8.5am Bristol to Weymouth, now worked by a twin set and intermediate trailer with the unusual situation that it called at Saltford, but not Keynsham. It was on one of the last legs of that daily roster that the twin set finally came to grief at St. Anne's Park when it caught fire and was gutted on 10th April 1956 whilst working the 9.8pm all stations from Bath to Bristol.

From the point of view of the railway enthusiast, the most interesting trains were the Swindon running in turns: engines of new construction or just out from overhaul were run in on a variety of stopping services from Swindon. The regular trains through Keynsham

Streamlined AEC internal combustion railcars leaving Keynsham and Somerdale for Bristol at 4.10pm on Sunday 18th May 1958. W23W leading W25W.   *Author*

Britannia pacific 70022 *Tornado* on the 10.5am from Bristol to Bath at Keynsham and Somerdale on 1st July 1957. A Swindon running-in duty.   *Author*

Newly constructed 5017 *St Donats Castle* at St Anne's Park being run in on a down service from Swindon, June 1932.   *H.W.Adams*

7015 *Carn Brea Castle* approaching Saltford station on 23rd November 1957 on the 10.05am Swindon running in duty.   *Hugh Ballantyne*

were for the larger main line engines and post war the timings were as follows:

    7.35am Swindon to Bristol calling at 8.57am
*10.05am Bristol to Bath   10.15am
 11.23am Bath to Swindon
    5.0pm Swindon to Bristol   6.33pm
    8.25pm Bristol to Swindon   8.35pm

*fifteen minutes later on Saturdays.

The newly painted gleaming engines normally worked for three consecutive days prior to dispatch back to their home sheds. During the currency of the winter timetable the same engine worked both the morning and evening trains, except on Saturdays, when a different one turned up in the evening. During the summer service it was a different one on the evening train within each three day cycle. There was a major surprise on 25th March 1957 when the famous *City of Truro* appeared for a three day stint on what was, undoubtedly, its first public outing since withdrawal in 1931 and incarceration in the then York Railway Museum. The 1957 overhaul at Swindon

restored the engine to main line running condition. (*City of Truro* created a world record for steam in May 1904 when it allegedly exceeded 100mph down Wellington bank, West of Taunton.)

Ex-works tank engines appeared erratically on the 4.7pm stopping service from Swindon (Keynsham 5.34pm), returning next day on the 1.10pm (SX) 1.25pm (SO) from Bristol to Bath, where it stood until 2.15pm (SX) or 2.21pm (SO) en route back to Swindon. The roster was very unusual for a train worked by tank engines being on alternate days a Swindon or Bristol Bath Road duty.

Finally, there was the 1.30pm (SO) from Chippenham to Bristol, an unbalanced working, which occasionally produced an ex-works tank engine making its way back to its depot in the West of England.

The timings quoted in the foregoing are from the author's post war experience, although the practice of running in engines on passenger work to Bristol goes back well into history. The practice came to a speedy end early in 1959 when the trains in question were taken over by DMUs. The end was abrupt, steam on Saturday - DMU on Monday morning. Steam did, however, reappear during the currency of the Summer timetables of 1960 and 1961, but only on Saturday afternoons. The steam rosters did last long enough to permit a few main line diesels to appear on the workings.

In 1953 the 4-4-0 Dukedog 9020 appeared in the area, in all probability working out its mileage prior to withdrawal. It was allocated to Swindon, returning home from Temple Meads at 5.45pm via Badminton, but it also appeared at Keynsham for a short while working the 6.25pm all stations to Chippenham.

Winter Service 1909-10

By 1909, Keynsham village had expanded by the provision of good quality terraced housing, much of it in roads off the High Street. There were also substantially built stone villas for the benefit of affluent Bristolians who wanted the good clean country air. They were the forerunners of a veritable multitude of travellers who we, to-day, refer to as commuters. So, since the date of the 1876 timetable there had been a considerable expansion in the service The working day was much longer than to-day, evidenced by the series of evening trains from Bristol, calling at 6.18 for Westbury, 6.30 for Swindon and 6.57 for Frome bringing toilers home from the City.

On the other hand, there is evidence of recreational activity with the 1.29pm extended to Saltford on Saturdays. The station there was adjacent to a popular site beside the river bank. However, on weekdays there was only one through train each day from Bristol to Weymouth which departed from Bristol at the very early and inconvenient time of 6 o'clock. Sunday was much better-out from Keynsham at 10.13am and back in the evening at 8.48. Nevertheless, it has to be remembered that Sunday trips to the seaside were just not done in 1910.

Fifteen services each week-day were worked by rail motor cars (one class only) and almost 50% of the Sunday service. It is difficult over 80 years later to determine how many were steam motor cars and how many were auto

fitted locomotives with trailers. Almost certainly the 9.53pm through Keynsham would have stabled overnight at Bath to work the first train in the morning back to Bristol and almost certainly it would have been of the rail motor variety, bearing in mind the likely patronage at those hours of the day.

A well established feature of the timetable was the through trains between Bristol and Reading via Devizes, a practice which survived until the complete closure of the Devizes loop in April 1966. During the currency of the timetable under review the down train called to set down at Keynsham upon request from passengers travelling from beyond Bath. Rather extraordinary, the same applied to a purely local train which started from Westbury and called about 3.25 in the afternoon.

Finally, there was a train which called at 8.23am through to Portsmouth and Southsea which survived right through to the day that the Keynsham service was decimated in 1970, although by then the train went no further than Salisbury.

Winter Service 1933-34

Here we have the Fry's worker trains depicted and which are identified by italics. The timings were very similar to those which survived through the 1959 dieselisation experiment and beyond. The ultimate run down is described in some detail in Chapter 8. The one major variation between 1933/4 and later years was the provision of trains for Saturday morning working pre-war, shown up by the Saturdays only return trains from Keynsham at 12.12, 12.17 and 12.45.

There was still the 8.21am to Portsmouth and Southsea. By now a corresponding return train is shown as calling at Keynsham at 6.8pm and that survived until dieselisation in 1959. There was still the 6 o'clock from Bristol to Weymouth and an additional train from Bristol at 5.3pm, but neither called at Keynsham.

Also there was still one rail motor service in each direction, a 4.11pm to Trowbridge and, in the other direction a 9.53pm from Swindon. No doubt, a part of a rostering jigsaw which got one train set off maintenance, balanced by another set coming in for maintenance.

There was a train which called at Keynsham at 9.42am which was the 8.40 from Chippenham via Melksham. It used the north to west side of the triangle at Bradford Junction (the other side goes to Trowbridge). The triangle was notable because one signal box served all three junctions. The route for the only passenger train of the day to use the curve provided a by-pass to the Box tunnel, used on occasions when the tunnel was closed for maintenance, permitting diverted trains to still call at all major stations between Bristol and Paddington. These days when those conditions apply, trains are diverted between Bath and Reading via the Hawkeridge curve and the Berks and Hants line. Unfortunates who wish to travel to Chippenham, Swindon or Didcot are directed to bus connections. Returning to the 9.40 at Keynsham, it was a means of keeping Bristol enginemen familiar with the route.

Two interesting trains were a down train calling at 7.53pm on week-days from Westbury, which can be traced through the timetable as running to Wells via Yatton which made it almost a circular service. The second, in the opposite direction started from Wells on Sundays which called at Keynsham at 8.46pm en route to Bath. It returned from Bath to Bristol at 9.31.

Winter Services 1952 - 53

Almost twenty years on from the winter service of 1933/4 the timetable for the winter of 1952/3 shows a remarkable similarity with that which went before, and that despite the war time cut backs and their subsequent restoration. The significant changes between the two timetables can be summarised as:

1. The disappearance of the Fry's trains which accommodated Saturday morning working.
2. There was now no evening train to Clifton Down for Fry' employees. Passengers would need to change at Stapleton Road.
3. There was now a train in both directions via Melksham.
4. The appearance in the timetable of services rostered for a diesel rail car.
5. Only the down trains on Sundays show a significant change in the pattern of' service.

Brush D0260 *Lion* on a test train passing St Anne's Park Station.   *Terry Nicholls*

WINTER SERVICE 1909-10

Up Trains		From	Time at Keynsham	To
WEEKDAYS				
		Bristol	6.10am	Weymouth
		Bristol	6.48	Swindon
		Bristol	7.33	Bath
		Bristol	8.23	Portsmouth Town
	m	Bristol	8.43	Chippenham
		Bristol	9.27	Frome
	m	Bristol	10.02	Bath
		Bristol	10.15	Westbury
		Bristol	11.13	Swindon
		Bristol	11.58	Bath
	m	Bristol	12.47pm	Bath
	m	Bristol	1.29	Keynsham (Saltford SO)
		Bristol	1.53	Bath
	m	Bristol	2.46	Bath
		Bristol	4.18	Reading via Devizes
	m	Bristol	4.42	Bath
		Bristol	5.28	Chippenham
		Bristol	6.18	Westbury
		Bristol	6.30	Swindon
		Bristol	6.57	Frome
		Bristol	7.48	Westbury
		Bristol	9.14	Trowbridge
	m	Bristol	9.53	Bath (Returned from Bath 6.15 next morning)
		Bristol	10.33	Bath
		Bristol	11.11	Trowbridge (Frome SO)
SUNDAYS				
		Bristol	10.13am	Weymouth
	m	Bristol	1.23pm	Bath
	m	Bristol	3.18	Trowbridge
		Bristol	3.58	Reading via Devizes
	m	Bristol	4.53	Trowbridge
		Bristol	6.12	Swindon
	m	Bristol	6.42	Westbury
		Bristol	9.54	Bath

Down Trains		From	Time at Keynsham	To	
WEEKDAYS					
	m	Bath	6.30am	Bristol	
	m	Chippenham	7.22	Bristol	
	m	Frome	8.02	Bristol	
		Bath	8.35	Bristol	
		Swindon	9.13	Bristol	
		Westbury	9.51	Bristol	
		Swindon	10.59	Bristol	
		Weymouth	11.26	Bristol	
	m	Bath	12.05pm	Bristol	
		Reading via Devizes	12.25 c	Bristol	(Sets down on request passsengers from beyond Bath)
		Bath	1.11	Bristol	
		Westbury	1.28	Bristol	
	m	Bath	2.02	Bristol	
	m	Keynsham	2.35	Bristol	
		Bath	3.00	Bristol	
		Westbury (Frome SO)	3.25 c	Bristol	ditto
		Bath	4.13	Bristol	
		Bath	5.17	Bristol	(arrives Keynsham at 5.03pm)
	m	Bath	6.38	Bristol	
		Bath	7.35	Bristol	
	m	Trowbridge	9.08	Bristol	
		Swindon	9.34	Bristol	
		Weymouth	10.11	Bristol	
		Bath	11.21	Bristol	
SUNDAYS					
	m	Bath	10.16am	Bristol	
	m	Trowbridge	1.12pm	Bristol	
	m	Trowbridge	2.20	Bristol	
		Bath	3.49	Bristol	
	m	Bath	5.36	Bristol	
		Swindon	7.27	Bristol	
		Weymouth	8.48	Bristol	
		Bath	9.54	Bristol	
		Bath	10.40	Bristol	

c	Approximate times only
m	Rail Motor Car (one class only)

WINTER SERVICE 1933–4

Up Trains	From	Time at Keynsham	To
WEEKDAYS			
	Parson Street	5.39am	Bath
	Bedminster	6.21	Bath
	Bristol	6.56	Swindon
	Parson Street	*7.27*	*Bath*
	Horfield	*7.32*	*Keynsham*
	Bristol	8.01	Bath
	Bristol	8.21	Portsmouth & Southsea
	Clifton Down	*8.36*	*Keynsham*
	Bristol	8.41	Bath
	Weston-super-Mare	8.56	Bath
	Bristol	9.56	Chippenham
	Bristol	10.39	Bath
	Bristol	11.53	Westbury
	Bristol	12.39pm	Bath
	Bristol	12.51	Westbury
	Severn Beach	*1.15 SX*	*Keynsham*
	Bristol	1.21 SX	Bath
	Bristol	1.39 SO	Bath
	Bristol	2.38	Bath
	Weston-super-Mare	2.56	Reading via Devizes
	Bedminster	4.11 m	Trowbridge (m = Rail Motor Car)
	Bristol	4.25	Chippenham
	Bristol	*4.50 SX*	*Keynsham*
	Bristol	5.29	Trowbridge
	Bristol	5.41	Chippenham
	Bristol	6.01 SX	Bath
	Bristol	6.26	Westbury
	Bristol	7.08	Salisbury
	Bristol	8.21	Swindon
	Bristol	9.16	Bath
	Bristol	10.01	Trowbridge
	Bristol	11.11	Westbury
SUNDAYS			
	Bedminster	8.41am	Bath
	Bristol	10.11	Westbury
	Bristol	1.18pm	Didcot
	Bristol	3.43	Portsmouth & Southsea
	Bristol	4.51	Bath
	Bristol	6.36	Trowbridge
	Bristol	7.19	Bath
	Wells via Yatton	8.46	Bath
	Bristol	10.17	Bath

Fry's worker trains shown in italics

WINTER SERVICE 1933–4

Down Trains From	Time at Keynsham	To
WEEKDAYS		
Bath	5.26am	Bristol
Bath	6.37	Bristol
Bath	7.15	Bristol
Westbury	7.52	Bristol
Bath	8.10	Parson Street
Westbury	8.39	Bristol
Swindon	8.57	Bristol
Chippenham via Devizes	9.42	Bristol
Bath	10.21	Torquay & Paignton
Swindon	10.39	Bristol
Keynsham	*12.12pm SO*	*Filton Junction*
Keynsham	*12.17 SO*	*Parson Street*
Chippenham	12.38	Weston-super-Mare
Keynsham	*12.45 SO*	*Clifton Down*
Trowbridge	1.40	Bristol (Bedminster SO)
Keynsham	*2.12 SX*	*Stapleton Road*
Swindon	2.18	Taunton
Salisbury	2.46	Bedminster
Trowbridge	3.36	Bristol
Chippenham	4.36	Bristol
Swindon	5.24	Bristol
Keynsham	*5.32 SX*	*Clifton Down*
Keynsham	*5.36 SX*	*North Filton Platform*
Keynsham	*5.44 SX*	*Parson Street*
Portsmouth & Southsea	6.08	Bristol
Newbury (via Devizes)	6.53	Bristol
Chippenham	7.39 SX	Bedminster
Westbury	7.53	Wells via Yatton
Swindon	9.33 m	Bristol (m = Rail Motor Car)
Bath	10.18	Bedminster
Swindon	11.04	Bristol
SUNDAYS		
Bath	10.16am	Bristol
Portsmouth & Southsea	2.01	Bristol
Trowbridge	5.07	Bristol
Bath	5.47	Bristol
Bath	8.11	Bristol
Swindon	8.42	Weston-super-Mare
Bath	9.31	Bristol
Bath	10.56	Bristol

Fry's worker trains shown in italics

WINTER SERVICE 1952-3

Up Trains	From	Time at Keynsham	To
WEEKDAYS			
	Bristol	5.38am	Bath
	Bristol	6.21	Bath
	Bristol	6.52	Swindon
	Parson Street	*7.23*	*Bath*
	North Filton Platform	*7.34*	*Westbury* (Arr Keynsham 7.27)
	Bristol	8.04	Bath (Formed 8.42 to Chippenham)
	Bristol	8.20	Portsmouth & Southsea
	Avonmouth Dock	*8.26 SX*	*Keynsham*
	Bristol	8.41	Bath
*	Bristol	10.15	Bath (Formed 11.25 to Swindon)
	Bristol	12.33pm	Bath
	Bristol	12.55	Bath
	Severn Beach	*1.16 SX*	*Keynsham*
**	*Parson Street*	*1.20 SX*	*Bath* (Formed 2.16 to Chippenham)
**	Bristol	1.35 SO	Bath (Formed 2.21 to Chippenham)
	Bristol	2.30	Bath (Formed 3.40 to Chippenham)
	Weston-super-Mare	2.48	Reading via Devizes
	Bristol	4.05	Melksham (SX), Trowbridge (SO)
	Bristol	4.43	Portsmouth & Southsea
	Bristol	*5.21*	*Trowbridge*
	Bristol	5.42	Chippenham
	Bristol	6.02	Westbury
	Bristol	6.35	Chippenham
	Bristol	7.20	Salisbury
	Bristol	8.05	Bath (Diesel Rail Car)
*	Bristol	8.35	Swindon
	Weston-super-Mare	9.41	Swindon
	Bristol	10.37 SO	Chippenham
	Bristol	11.10	Westbury
SUNDAYS			
	Bristol	8.40am	Chippenham
	Bristol	10.20	Weymouth
	Bristol	12.05pm	Bath (Diesel Rail Car)
	Bristol	1.15	Swindon
	Bristol	2.40	Trowbridge
	Weston-super-Mare	3.42	Westbury
	Bristol	4.45	Bath
	Bristol	6.45	Bath
	Bristol	8.52	Swindon
	Bristol	10.29	Bath

Down Trains	From	Time at Keynsham	To
WEEKDAYS			
	Bath	5.28am	Bristol
	Bath	6.29	Bristol
	Bath	*7.15*	*Taunton*
	Westbury	7.50	Bristol
	Bath	8.14	Bristol
	Trowbridge	8.39	Taunton
*	Swindon	8.57	Bristol
	Chippenham (via Melksham)	9.40	Bristol
	Bath	10.23	Bristol
	Swindon	10.48	Bristol
	Portsmouth & Southsea	11.57	Bristol
	Chippenham	12.38pm	Bristol
	Westbury	1.39	Bristol
	Keynsham	*2.15 SX*	*Stapleton Road*
	Swindon	2.30	Bristol
	Portsmouth & Southsea	2.54	Bristol
	Westbury	4.51	Bristol
	Keynsham	*5.25 SX*	*Henbury*
	Keynsham	*5.28 SX*	*Parson Street*
**	Swindon	5.34	Bristol
	Portsmouth & Southsea	6.05	Bristol
*	Swindon	6.35	Bristol
	Chippenham	7.59 SO	Bristol
	Trowbridge	8.40	Bristol (8.45 FO)
	Bath	9.21	Bristol (Diesel Rail Car)
	Keynsham	*10.14 SX*	*Bristol* (Diesel Rail Car – unadvertised)
	Westbury	10.43	Bristol
	Bath	11.23 SO	Bristol
SUNDAYS			
	Bath	10.14am	Bristol
	Bath	1.04pm	Bristol (Diesel Rail Car)
	Challow	3.12	Bristol
	Trowbridge	4.34	Bristol
	Bath	5.32	Bristol
	Swindon	6.35	Bristol
	Bath	7.54	Bristol
	Swindon	9.08	Bristol
	Westbury	10.01	Bristol
	Bath	11.15	Bristol

*   Regular Swindon running in duties
** Occasional Swindon running in duty
    Fry's worker trains shown in italics

7029 *Clun Castle* approaches Keynsham and Somerdale whilst hauling the last through steam train from Paddington to Bristol on 27th November 1965. Steam ceased on the Western Region (except for the Somerset and Dorset) at the end of 1965. *Author*

To conclude this chapter it may be appropriate to refer to the changeover from steam to other forms of traction. The variety of prototypes which could be seen working through Keynsham was one of the facets of that changeover, encompassing multiple units as well as both passenger and freight locomotives.

Before dieselisation became a serious main line proposition, the pre-nationalisation big four were progressing their own projects. The GWR opted for gas turbines. Although ordered before nationalisation, the Swiss Brown-Boveri design did not appear until 1950 as 18000, the Metropolitan Vickers not until December 1951 as 18100. Both locomotives, when

Prototype HST power car 43001 on a Research Department special train at Keynsham on 13th May 1978, eighteen months after withdrawal from main line passenger work. *Author*

available, were frequent performers on the. Bristol to Paddington services. Both ceased work before the end of the decade.

The early days produced no fewer than seven varieties of prototype and manufacturer's demonstration locomotive designs working through Keynsham. Of those, the Brush 0280 *Falcon* (later BR1200) was the longest in service. Constructed in 1961, it arrived at Bristol Bath Road in February 1965 and was put to work, when it was in good health, on the London trains. It finished its days in South Wales until withdrawal in 1975.

Lion, a product of the Birmingham Railway Carriage and Wagon Company, had a short life of 18 months (1962/3). For a short time it could be seen on the 11.15am from Paddington to Bristol as well as on test trains.

In a slightly different vein D1733 (later 47614, then 47853) was painted in an experimental blue livery in 1964, and for publicity purposes only was photographed attached to the then new XP64 coaching stock,

the prototype for the Mk2 design. D1733, being an Old Oak Common allocated locomotive was frequently seen in the Bristol area and, initially, the first and only one in the new corporate livery, although in a lighter shade of blue than finally adopted.

Turning to multiple units, a very early design was the three car C1.126 units, constructed at Swindon in 1956/7. It has been said that almost every form of motive power ever constructed at Swindon would appear, in due course, on the main line to Bristol. They were no exception. Although destined for Scotland, and in particular for the Edinburgh to Glasgow expresses, some of the running-in was done on the line to Bristol via Bath.

Two years later, in 1959, marked the arrival of the Bristol Pullman, running between Bristol and Paddington, again, when it was in good health. For occasions when not so, the Western Region assembled a motley collection of old locomotive hauled Pullman cars still in their familiar traditional livery and they alone were

Standard 2–6–2T, newly constructed, on the 1.15pm (SO) Bristol to Bath running in duty, arriving at Keynsham and Somerdale on 25th June 1955.   *Author*

an innovation in the area, hauled by a diesel hydraulic of the Warship class. The Pullman sets were dogged with two problems, unreliable engines and poor riding characteristics. Nevertheless, for the privilege of travelling by Pullman a supplementary fare was charged, even for the short eleven miles between Bristol and Bath. The Pullmans are included in this chapter because they were the forerunners of the HSTs

The prototype HST 252 001 commenced regular revenue service on the Bristol to London main line via Bath on 5th May 1975, but only survived in that capacity for just eighteen months, by which time the production HSTs were coming on stream. For that short period of time passengers had the unique opportunity to experience the dawn of high speed train travel, unique to the Bristol to London line and with no supplement to pay.

On the freight side, there arrived at St Philip's Marsh in 1959 an 0-6-0 DE shunter constructed two years previously by the Vulcan Foundry as D0226. It survived for twelve

months before returning to its birthplace. It was employed mainly on the afternoon Bristol to Chippenham goods and return. D0226 can now be seen in preservation. on the Keighley and Worth Valley Railway.

A similar machine, but in 0-8-0 configuration arrived at the Marsh in 1961 from the Yorkshire Engine Company, named *Taurus*. That only stayed about twelve months and, like D0226 was employed mainly on the Chippenhem goods.

In short, Keynsham station was a very good spot for enthusiasts to see locomotives and trains, both passenger and freight, in action, rather than stationary in a station or idle on a depot.

The 15th July 1959 was a red letter day Dieselisation was complete at Bristol and a new timetable was introduced. There were booklets setting out the new augmented services throughout the Bristol Division. The copy read:

"These diesel trains have been specially designed for speed and comfort. Their technical capabilities, particularly their capacity

Prototype DH 0–8–0 *Taurus* from the Yorkshire Engine Co stables in the Keynsham down loop on the return Chippenham goods. 25th July 1961.   *Author*

for acceleration will provide an improvement over previous services.

The pleasing interior decoration, comfortable seating accommodation and a modern system of heating and ventilation to counteract extremes of temperature, provide an up-to-date and attractive travel service."

We may not recognise that glowing description in to-day's clapped out survivors, but it was true enough in its day.

On Mondays to Fridays there were no fewer than 34 up trains from Bristol and 32 in the down, with a half hourly frequency at Keynsham for much of the day. So lavish was it that there was a half hourly service to late in the evening, as set out below:

8.5pm	Bristol to	Swindon
8.35pm	"	Trowbridge
9.5pm	"	Chippenham
9.35pm	'	Trowbridge
10.5pm	Bristol to	Swindon
10.35pm	"	Trowbridge
11.5pm	"	Chippenham
11.35pm	"	Bath

On Sunday there were 17 trains calling at Keynsham, starting very early with the 7.30am from Bristol, followed by another at 8.25am. There were 13 trains in the opposite direction. It is not surprising that most of such trains ran nearly empty.

Apart from three up trains, one down, the Frys' employee trains and the summer only excursion from Swindon to Weston-super-Mare, all trains were operated with the new dmus.

The railway persevered with the timetable for nearly three years, but such were the losses that a much reduced and more realistic timetable was introduced on 5th March 1962, not waiting for the expiration of the then current timetable on 17th June. A report in the Daily Telegraph put forth the situation concisely, and fairly and is reproduced below:

"Cuts of nearly one third in train services in the Bristol area, intended to save about £250,000 a year were announced yesterday. Western Region of British Rail said that of the 2292 trains per week, nearly 800 would be discontinued. Only principal stations would remain open on

Sundays and about 30 smaller stations would close at 7.30pm. Mr D.S. Hart, Divisional Traffic Manager said the new services would start on 5th March, but it is still not certain that they would pay. If they were not well patronised further cuts would be necessary.

Mr Hart said that the Region had high hopes when a more intensive train service was introduced in 1959 to coincide with the advent of diesels. The service, which represented an increase in train mileage of 42%, was started with the help of every publicity medium. He added: "the public has not responded. This is, no doubt, accounted for by the rapid increase in private transport and the lessening of evening travel due to changing social habits, such as television."

A frequent rail service during the middle of the day and evenings was not necessary. Only 44 trains, or 2%, carried a satisfactory load of more than 60 passengers. About 74% ran with less than 20 passengers and it was not unknown for some diesel trains operated by a staff of two to have only a single passenger. In fact, 1,700 local trains failed to cover the cost of running them."

Perhaps, the most significant reason for the failure was the inconvenient location of Temple Meads station in relation to the commercial and shopping centres of Bristol, almost a mile distant. At that period too, there was a ten minute frequency of buses between Bristol and Bath, increased to every 7½ minutes on Saturday afternoons.

As far as Keynsham was concerned, the number of trains calling was reduced to a still respectable seventeen up and fifteen down on week-days. The late evening trains disappeared completely, so that the last to Bristol was at 7.22pm, and the last to Bath at 8.8pm. Keynsham was also one of the 30 smaller stations to lose its Sunday service.

The revised and reduced train service at Keynsham remained basically untouched until the end of the decade when an attempt was made to close the station completely. That story is narrated in chapter 8.

SUMMER SERVICE 1959 - WEEKDAYS

Up Trains	From	Time at Keynsham	To	
	Parson Street	5.40am	Bath	
	Bristol	6.25	Bath	
	Bristol	6.52	Swindon	Steam
	Parson Street	*7.23*	*Bath*	
	North Filton Platform	*7.34*	*Westbury* arr 7.27	Steam
	Bristol	8.00	Chippenham	
	Bristol	8.20	Salisbury	Steam
	Avonmouth Dock	*8.26*	*Keynsham*	Steam
	Bristol	8.45	Chippenham	
	Bristol	9.15	Bath	
	Bristol	10.15	Swindon	
	Bristol	10.45	Trowbridge	
	Bristol	11.15	Swindon	
	Bristol	12.15pm	Chippenham	
	Bristol	12.45	Trowbridge	
	Bristol	1.15	Chippenham	
	Bristol	1.45	Westbury	
	Bristol	2.20	Chippenham	
	Bristol	3.15	Chippenham	
	Bristol	3.45	Melksham	
	Bristol	4.45	Weymouth	
	Bristol	*5.21*	*Westbury*	
	Bristol	5.45	Chippenham	
	Bristol	6.01	Trowbridge	Steam
	Bristol	6.45	Chippenham	
	Bristol	7.10	Bath	
	Bristol	8.15	Swindon	
	Bristol	8.45	Westbury	
	Bristol	9.15	Chippenham	
	Bristol	9.45	Westbury	
	Bristol	10.15	Swindon	
	Bristol	10.45	Westbury	
	Bristol	11.15	Chippenham	
	Bristol	11.45	Bath	

Fry's worker trains shown in italics

SUMMER SERVICE 1959 - WEEKDAYS

Down Trains	From	Time at Keynsham	To	
	Bath	5.29am	Bristol	
	Bath	6.29	Bristol	
	Bath	7.14	Bristol	
	Swindon	7.31	Taunton	
	Frome	7.49	Bristol	
	Bath	8.14	Bristol	
	Westbury	8.39	Taunton	Steam
	Swindon	8.54	Bristol	
	Chippenham	9.41	Bristol	(via Melksham)
	Swindon	9.49	Weston-super-Mare Locking Road (29th Jun until 28th Aug) Steam	
	Swindon	11.09	Weston-super-Mare General	
	Westbury	11.45	Bristol	
	Bath	12.10pm	Bristol	
	Bath	12.45	Bristol	
	Westbury	1.40	Bristol	
	Swindon	2.08	Weston-super-Mare General	
	Trowbridge	2.40	Bristol	
	Westbury	3.40	Bristol	
	Westbury	4.40	Bristol	
	Keynsham	*5.25*	*Henbury*	Steam
	Bath	*5.28*	*Parson Street*	Steam
	Swindon	5.34	Bristol	
	Westbury	6.12	Bristol	
	Swindon	6.25	Bristol	
	Westbury	6.51	Bristol	
	Weymouth	7.40	Bristol	
	Chippenham	8.06	Bristol	
	Westbury	8.55	Bristol	
	Chippenham	10.10	Bristol	
	Trowbridge	10.40	Bristol	
	Swindon	11.11	Bristol	
	Bath	11.40	Bristol	

Fry's worker trains shown in italics

SUMMER SERVICE 1959 – SUNDAYS

Up Trains	From at Keynsham	Time	To	
Bristol	7.40am	Chippenham	Steam	
Bristol	8.35	Westbury		
Bristol	10.00	Weymouth	Steam	
Bristol	10.20	Weymouth	Steam	
Bristol	10.55	Bath		
Bristol	12.15pm	Bath		
Bristol	1.10	Chippenham		
Bristol	1.55	Bath		
Bristol	2.40	Trowbridge		
Bristol	3.50	Weymouth		
Bristol	5.05	Bath		
Bristol	6.20	Bath		
Weston-super-Mare Locking Road	7.12	Swindon	Steam (not after 30th Aug)	
Bristol	9.00	Swindon		
Bristol	9.23	Warminster		
Weston-super-Mare General	9.52	Chippenham		
Bristol	10.45	Bath		

Down Trains	From	Time at Keynsham	To	
	Bath	9.24am	Bristol	
	Westbury	10.06	Weston-super-Mare General	
	Chippenham	10.40	Bristol	Steam
	Bath	11.40	Bristol	
	Bath	1.05pm	Bristol	
	Chippenham	3.05	Bristol	
	Trowbridge	4.30	Bristol	
	Swindon	5.33	Weston-super-Mare General	
	Westbury	8.02	Bristol	
	Swindon	9.02	Bristol	
	Weymouth	9.31	Bristol	Steam
	Weymouth	9.54	Bristol	Steam
	Westbury	11.18	Bristol	

REVISED SERVICE
5th MARCH – 17th JUNE 1962 - WEEKDAYS

Up Trains	From	Time at Keynsham	To
	Bristol	5.40am	Bath
	Bristol	6.25	Bath
	Filton Junction	6.33	Swindon
	Weston-super-Mare General	*7.25*	*Paddington*
	Avonmouth Dock	*7.33*	*Westbury*
	Bristol	7.50	Chippenham
	Bristol	8.28	Salisbury
	Bristol	8.40	Chippenham
	Bristol	12.45pm	Bath
	Bristol	2.45 SO	Chippenham
	Bristol	3.33	Swindon
	Bristol	4.05	Melksham SX, Trowbridge SO
	Bristol	4.34	Weymouth
	Bristol	5.31	Westbury
	Bristol	5.45	Calne
	Bristol	6.05	Westbury
	Bristol	7.22	Salisbury

Down Trains	From	Time at Keynsham	To
	Bath	5.29	Bristol
	Bath	6.29	Taunton
	Bath	*7.14*	*Bristol*
	Swindon	7.31	Taunton
	Frome	8.00	Bristol
	Westbury	8.40	Bristol
	Swindon	8.56	Bristol
	Calne	9.41	Bristol via Melksham
	Chippenham	11.18 SX	Bristol
	Portsmouth & Southsea	*12.55pm*	*Cardiff*
	Weymouth	1.39	Bristol
	Keynsham	*4.10 FO*	*Henbury*
	Keynsham	*4.17 FO*	*Parson Street*
	Westbury	4.40	Bristol
	Bath	*5.15 SX*	*Henbury*
	Chippenham	*5.23*	*Parson Street*
	Westbury	6.15	Bristol
	Calne	8.08 SO	Bristol

No Sunday Service
Fry's worker trains shown in italics

6. Fry's Private Siding

A small souvenir booklet given to every visitor to Somerdale in the early post war years summarises the early days of the chocolate firm as follows:

"The Firm of J.S. Fry & Sons Ltd., was founded in Bristol in the first half of the 18th century by Dr Joseph Fry, a Quaker physician with wide scientific and commercial interests. He bought a small shop which had been established in 1728 by Mr Walter Churchman, and with it he acquired patent rights and recipes for the manufacture of drinking chocolate.

In 1777 the business was removed to Union Street, then a new and fashionable thoroughfare. To Dr Fry's shop came the "Quality", the rich and the elegant. In those days chocolate was very much of a luxury. It was drunk by the merchant princes of Bristol and their wives and daughters and was the modish drink for the aristocracy who thronged the Pump Room at Bath. Dr Fry was succeeded as head of the business by his wonderful wife Anna, and then by their son, Joseph Storrs Fry, who was the first chocolate manufacturer to introduce factory methods into the industry."

From that small beginning, the firm of J.S. Fry & Sons developed, and with it the conglomeration of factories and ancillary premises which occupied a congested site which now forms part of the present day Broadmead Shopping Centre. By the beginning of the 20th Century the factories were hemmed in on all sides, added to which (as one internal report stated) all the finished products had to be carted to the various railway depots such as Canons Marsh, Temple Meads, Pylle Hill and St Philips. After the end of World War I a search began in earnest for completely new premises on a green field site where good transport facilities could be easily made available. That search culminated in what became known as Somerdale, adjacent to the then small market town of Keynsham, some five miles from the Bristol city centre. An important factor in the choice of Somerdale

was the availability of road, rail and water transport modes and the adjacent railway passenger station for the employees.

The nearby River Avon was seriously considered as a mode to bring in bulk cocoa beans, sugar and coal with transhipment from sea going vessels to lighters at Avonmouth for onward transport to a new wharf adjacent to the new factory. The river management was (and still is) in the hands of the Port of Bristol Authority as far as Hanham lock, and beyond there the GWR. (The GWR inherited responsibility for the canalised river from Hanham to Bath when they took over the Kennet and Avon Canal back in 1852)

A Fry's Board Report in 1921 makes mention of visits by senior personnel to the offices of the undermentioned for consultation with a view to ascertaining possibilities:

Forward Lighterage Company, Bristol
Messrs Benj Perry and Sons, Bristol
Mr G.T. Beard, Lighterman, Gloucester
The Port of Bristol Authority. (PBA)

All the parties showed interest in the proposals, especially the PBA, although there were reservations concerning the cost of transhipment from seagoing vessel to lighter as it was thought that the dockers would be asking for more money. The lighterage concerns also pointed out that traffic was liable to disruption, particularly when the river was in flood. It was agreed by all parties that the river would require dredging on both sides of Hanham lock, but no difficulties were foreseen on that score. However, Hanham lock proved to be the obstacle that could not be overcome because of the restriction on the size of vessels which could use it. Furthermore, there would be considerable expense involved in the construction of especially designed craft and guarantees would be required as to the tonnage to be conveyed.

Fry's management were wary of the GWR, thinking that they may not be co-operative when finding that it was proposed to bring in most of the raw materials by water. That being so, the PBA, who shared the misgivings, offered to make some initial soundings. In the event, the railway proved most co-operative on the grounds that the more material that was brought in by water, the greater would be the traffic on offer to the railway in the form of finished products.

The Report to the Board of the meeting with the railway on 19th December 1921 contains much of interest and is reproduced verbatim.

"I met the Assistant District Manager of the GWR Bristol and so far as the dredging etc of the waterway from Hanham lock to Keynsham was concerned, he said that his Company would be quite prepared to meet us in the matter and suggested the best way to go into same would be for a joint inspection to be made of the river in the New Year between the representatives of the GWR and ourselves to find out exactly what is required and to make the river suitable to deal with loaded lighters which could pass Hanham lock.

I referred to correspondence which had taken place last year respecting rates for traffic to and from Keynsham and requested that the Rly Co (sic) would now consider the question of granting us Bristol Port rates and using them as a ground work upon which to base our exceptional rates. I pointed out to the Rly Co that there would be little work for them to do in connection with our private siding - simply putting in inwards loads and taking out our outwards traffic from a given point at a given time, and that we felt that rates should be based upon conveyance plus a small charge for shunting services rendered at the siding.

Whilst on the question of shunting, I would suggest that consideration be given to our using a small electric shunting engine after the type of that which has just been instituted by several of the leading Rly Cos in one or two of their principal goods yards, with considerable success. This type of locomotive is more convenient to work and less expensive, and is cleaner and lighter than a steam locomotive, and furthermore, only uses "fuel" when actually working; the advantage of such a vehicle is also felt by the fact that as it is not as heavy as the ordinary shunting engine,

the original permanent way expenses for sidings etc is less."

So, to the siding itself. At a Joint Board Meeting held in 1920 (Cadbury/Fry) expenditure up to £15,000 was authorised for siding accommodation

At a Bristol Board Meeting in 1921, the estimated cost of the Eastern approach siding was £5,915. (That would be from Station Hill to the GWR main line)

On 5th January 1921, the following report appeared in the Bristol Evening Times and Echo:

"At a meeting of the Somerset County Council yesterday an application was reported from Messrs J.S. Fry and Sons Ltd, for sanction to lay a railway siding across the main road adjoining Keynsham Station. They contemplated developing the Hams Estate at Keynsham, on lines comparable to those adopted by Messrs Cadbury Bros, at Bournville. An essential factor in the development of the estate was a railway connection which could only be made by means of the proposed level crossing. The committee recommended that no objection be taken to the proposal provided Messrs J.S. Fry and Sons Ltd undertake entire responsibility and agree to the following conditions: (1) That the road should be stopped twice a day for five minutes; (2) That the stoppages be at specified times; (3) That they should warn road traffic at their own expense during such stoppages, and that no gates should be erected across the main road.

Mr Willoughby (a Keynsham Parish Councillor) said he had taken the opinion of a great many people in Keynsham, and he found they were generally in favour of allowing Messrs Fry to have the crossing."

Work commenced on the construction of the siding in January 1922. The GWR laid the crossing on the high road in May 1923. The first commercial consignment to use the siding was on 17th January 1925.

The railway lines laid on the site made up 2½ miles of single track, 4,000 sleepers were laid and 9,000 tons of ashes were used. A photograph depicting construction of the

Construction of Fry's siding. *Courtesy Miss J. Knight*

siding appears above.

It was forbidden for the engine to propel its train in or out of the siding, that being so, it was necessary for the engine to run around its train after arrival from Bristol and before entering the factory siding. Likewise, after leaving the siding with the outward load, the engine had to run around its train prior to returning to Bristol. That was all because the siding connection to the main line faced the Bath direction instead of Bristol.

A notable engine regularly used on the transfer trains during the war years was No 6, the Stroudley "Terrier" acquired from the defunct Weston, Clevedon and Portishead Railway in 1940. Otherwise, in steam days, motive power was normally 0-6-0 pannier tanks. Following dieselisation the regular classes used were, successively 14, 22, 35 and 25

A considerable proportion of the inward traffic originated from the Avonmouth Docks in the form of sacks of cocoa beans and sugar. Outgoing traffic was almost wholly finished chocolate products which, most conveniently,

could be conveyed in the same trucks as had brought in the raw materials. A proportion of the outward traffic was consigned to rail connected distribution depots which were at strategic points up and down the country. An early official internal GWR report noted with some satisfaction that "The opening of this (first) section of the Factory has diverted a certain amount of goods traffic from Bristol, but in addition has secured to us all the competitive traffic, some of which would have found its way to the LMS Railway but for its new point of origin." No doubt, the LMS thought otherwise.

As soon as production started up in the new factory problems immediately began to arise at the station. Due to the sudden increase in the workload, the available workforce was unable to cope. In a report dated 11th March 1925, the number of outward invoices for the week ended 6th March was 703. The report then went on to say:

"All the traffic from the Factory is dealt with as "carriage paid" and about half of it is consigned to stations which require it to be dealt with as Railway Clearance House traffic (i.e. to stations off the GWR) At the present time only a few of the rates necessary are being put into operation and there are no fewer than 300 cases for January last and 950 for February under the "particulars to follow" process, which will involve a great deal of work to dispose of. The cases are likely to be even more for March and probably rebate allowances will be claimed in respect of them as well as others further multiplying the amount of clerical work. Claims are also beginning to arrive and 60 have been received at the station from the firm up to now"

In short, it was administrative chaos and it was no wonder that the Station Master was already claiming to be upgraded from Class 3 to Class 2.

Apparently, without waiting for authority from Paddington, the Bristol Divisional Superintendent, together with the Divisional Goods Manager, took it upon themselves to

appoint an additional clerk, and they also transferred a checker from Bristol, a man who already lived in Keynsham. That man was employed full time in the factory "for the purpose of checking consignments in connection with the charging and claims now arising, but also for the purpose of seeing that the loading into trucks is properly performed to reduce the amount of transfer work at Bristol and at other places to a minimum."

Traffic fell off very seriously during the 1970s as the firm became more and more road oriented. Latterly, one train per day sufficed to deal with the traffic on offer. The last train left the siding in September 1978. The Hudswell Clarke shunter was sold to scrap merchants T.W. Ward of Salford in 1979. They later moved it to Silvertown where it was cut up about 1987. The track was lifted in 1979 and some was transported to the nearby Bitton preservation site. Ten years on the cutting resembled a jungle.

British Rail lifted the track on their side of

Fry's Sentinel shunter as seen in its preserved condition at Bacton, Suffolk.   *R. Finbow*

Fry's second shunter, the Hunslet, seen at the factory's Station Hill crossing gates. Undated.

Cadbury Ltd

the road crossing during September 1979, although the actual rail connection into the main line was not taken out until July 1980. The shallow cutting has been filled in and the site incorporated into the new station car park.

Finally, one extraordinary item. In both the GWR and BR working timetables there are extensive lists of prohibitions for designated classes of engines on nominated lines, branches and sidings. The only prohibition for Fry's siding was the humble GWR diesel railcar of the 1930s which was not permitted on the loading bay curve. Even the mighty King class was presumably permitted, not that one ever ventured there.

To work the siding complex Fry's had their own shunting locomotive. The first one was a four wheel Sentinel, works number 7492 of 1928. That locomotive would agree somewhat loosely with the technically garbled description

in the Report referred to on page 68. It was sold to the Grove Iron and Steel Merchants in January 1964, but was subsequently purchased by Mr G.R. Finbow of Bacton Suffolk and it now carries the name *"FRY"*. According to a contemporary report in Fry's Magazine, on the occasion of its departure from Somerdale for scrap the Sentinel was plated by the GWR to authorise it "to chug across the Keynsham-Hanham Road". No reference to that authorisation has been found in such records as survive. According to the same report it had only two drivers, Joe Payne and Graham Hendy. However, it did chug across the Hanham Road on to GWR track, but only to collect (or deliver) the occasional van from the loading dock adjacent to the up main line platform. It never ventured on to the main line further than was necessary to perform the required shunting movement.

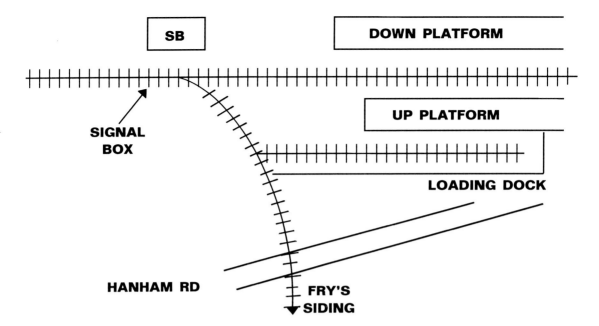

| SB | | DOWN PLATFORM |

SIGNAL
BOX

UP PLATFORM

LOADING DOCK

HANHAM RD — FRY'S
SIDING

Keynsham and the Fry's branch layout 1925-1979.

Class 22 D6349 with No 10 Transfer with traffic for Somerdale passing Bristol East Depot on 4th June 1968. The right hand up side yard is now occupied by the non-rail connected Unicorn Trading Estate. The down side yard has been taken over by the Engineers. *Author*

D0280 *Falcon* passing Keynsham and Somerdale on the 09.15 from Bristol to Paddington on 3rd August 1965. *Author*

The replacement for the Sentinel was an 0-4-0 diesel mechanical, built by Hudswell Clarke of Leeds, works number Dl009. It was purchased in 1956, eight years prior to the disposal of the Sentinel. There was also a narrow gauge 1ft 11¾in layout employing a four wheel Lister diesel (formerly petrol) shunter, makers number 8023 of 1936. The Lister hauled standard gauge coal wagons to the tippler in the power house by means of a capstan and cable attached to the wagons on the parallel track. It was sold to scrap merchants R.J. King of Farrington Gurney in 1972.

The amount of traffic entering and coming out of the siding was sufficient to require two trains each day, by what was latterly known as No 10 Transfer. According to the Working Timetable for Freight Trains in the Bristol District (November 1959 to June 1960) the trains were timed as follows:

Bristol East Depot	dpt	9.55am	1.15pm
Keynsham & Somerdale	arr	l0.10	1.27
"	dpt	l2.10	4.34
Bristol East Depot	arr	l2.27	
Bristol Temple Meads			4.40
(goods)			

The timetable meant that the train had to cross Station Hill four times each day on the level. For that manoeuvre two Fry's employees were deputed to stand in the middle of the road, one on each side of the line in order to hold up the road traffic.

7. Station Road Bridge and Station Hill

There were two areas of concern which involved the railway to which the Local Authorities of the day became very much aware long before the first bar of Five Boys ever left the production line.

The first concerned the level crossing, for barely two months after it had been laid in May 1923, the Bitton Parish Council was complaining about hold ups on Station Hill whilst railway trucks were shunted across the road. With the road transport industry very much in its infancy, virtually all the factory construction material was brought in by rail. There is photographic confirmatory evidence that most of it was shunted across Station Hill on to the factory site - hence the hold ups.

The second area for concern was the inadequacy of the Station Road railway bridge, but that only became one aspect of a wider embracing scheme, for the two Local Authorities immediately involved were waking up to the fact that something needed to be done about Station Hill. As we will see, nothing was done about Station Hill, but eventually the railway bridge was rebuilt. Four months before the crossing was laid, in January 1923, the Keynsham Rural District Council were asking Fry's to consider the widening of Station Hill "in view of the possible danger of the level crossing."

On the 10th September 1923, the Keynsham Parish Council minuted;

"That in view of the greatly increased heavy and fast moving traffic passing over Station Hill, this Parish Council are strongly of the opinion that steps should be taken to straighten the hill and widen the bridges at each end. The hill is serpentine in its course, the bends are awkward, railway metals cross at its middle and County Bridge is at an acute angle."

The Council minuted that the matter be brought to the attention of the Keynsham and Warmley Rural District Councils and the Somerset County Council. The Warmley Rural District Council was involved, and ultimately the Gloucestershire County Council because the River Avon and the County Bridge constituted the administrative boundary for the Counties of Gloucester and Somerset and each Authority had a 50% responsibility for the bridge.

The Keynsham Rural District Council were enthusiastic and passed the proposal to the Somerset County Council as highly commended and they, in turn, passed it to their Highways Committee who passed it on again to the Main Roads Sub-Committee.

On the other side of the River Avon the Warmley District Council were interested and passed the proposal on to the Gloucestershire County Council: they poured cold water on to the idea, saying that they would not be able to consider the scheme for at least twelve months. Nevertheless, Somerset persisted with the proposal and, in due course, Messrs Fry produced a most interesting plan which involved:

1. Widening the railway bridge in Station Road.
2. The abandonment of Station Hill for through traffic and in its place it was proposed to construct a new road having a wide sweep passing through where the Fry's main gates now stand, across the land used for the outdoor museum, a bridge over the siding (in a cutting at that point), and a direct approach to the County Bridge at its then position.

In March 1924 the Keynsham Rural District Council minuted:

"The Highway Surveyor reported that he had met the representative of the Ministry of Transport, the Divisional Engineer and the County Surveyor with Messrs Fry's representative and that the County Surveyor stated that the matter had been referred to the Main Roads Sub-Committee and that the Committee would further consider the matter when Messrs Fry had informed them what they would contribute towards the proposals in addition to giving up the land required for the improvement. Col. Stallard, representing the Ministry of Transport, stated that the proposed scheme was not

A view looking out of the factory gate towards the station with a horse box in the loading dock.

Cadbury Ltd

one that could be initiated by the Ministry of Transport and if it materialised it could only be done through the County Council."

The proposals were dropped in the following November when the Somerset County Council decided not to proceed having "committed themselves to an expense of £510,000 for Unemployment Relief Works on the Bristol and Exeter Main Road."

Nothing more happened for a few years except that Fry's, at their own expense, had one of the wing walls of the bridge rebuilt on the curve. The work was completed in December 1928. Then the railway decided that they wanted to lengthen the station platforms to better deal with the increased passenger traffic created by the influx of Fry's employees. More importantly, there was the need to better cater for the lengthy excursion trains, too long for the existing platforms and therefore, the

necessity to 'draw up', i.e. to draw forward to permit passengers in the rear coaches to alight. In order to effect the required improvement it was necessary to reconstruct the Station Road bridge - Measom's "Most handsome on the line". Authority for the work to be carried out was given in February 1930.

Without further delay, the railway approached the Somerset County Council to enquire whether they would like to avail themselves of the opportunity to increase the width of the roadway from 21 feet 6 inches to 40 feet between parapets. Having regard to the increasing quantity of traffic using the bridge in connection with J.S. Fry & Sons Ltd., the County Council, at their meeting in March 1930, agreed to a contribution of £3,000 towards the cost, provided the Ministry of Transport met 75% of the total cost. The County Council did not appear to demur when, at their meeting in June, the requested contribution was increased to £4,000, plus

The loading bay with the destinations for the traffic clearly indicated. *Cadbury Ltd*

A Dean 0–6–0 with what appears to be an early view of a No 10 transfer at the loading bay siding. *Cadbury Ltd*

76

A van plated to travel between Fry's Somerdale and Manchester Oldham Road.   *Cadbury Ltd*

£773, representing the capitalised cost' of maintenance and renewal.

The girders for the replacement bridge were put in place on Sunday 22nd November 1931 whilst single line working operated on the railway underneath.[1] With a new bridge in position, the railway soon got to work to lengthen the platforms to approximately 790 feet from an inadequate 383 feet on the up side and 430 feet on the down side. Included in the platform work carried out was the provision of unsightly corrugated iron roofing over a portion of the new platforms. Some of that remains to-day, the colander state of the ironwork providing a very uncertain shelter from the elements.

Once the platforms were lengthened, the two homegoing Fry's workers' trains were brought into the down platform, one behind the other. That dubious practice was changed when new crossovers were provided west of the station in July 1933, thus permitting both trains to be in the station at the same time, but one starting from the up platform.

To summarise, the Parish Council got a widened road bridge in Station Road, thanks to the Great Western Railway and not the Somerset County Council. They never got the requested improvement to the serpentine course of Station Hill, for the improved alignment through Fry's ground and a bridge over the siding never came to fruition. After a delay of 56 years, and thanks to nobody in particular, the level crossing became disused in 1979.

Nobody could have foreseen the disastrous flood of July 1968 which washed away the old County Bridge and which was replaced at some considerable cost by a new bridge on a much improved alignment. This time the Gloucestershire County Council had to be involved whether they wanted to or not.

It is convenient at this point to refer to the Avon Road gates. The continuation of Avon Road from the goods yard gates to its junction with the bottom of Station Hill was a railway owned private road. There were cast iron notices to that effect displayed at each end which, of course, everybody ignored until.......In the exercise of its rights, the railway closed the road each year on Christmas Day to both pedestrians and motorists. At dusk on Christmas Eve the Station Master locked the gates across the road at the Station Hill end, leaving an oil lamp showing red hanging from the said gates. No other warning was given to motorists who, coming upon the closed gates had little room to manoeuvre in order to reverse. An entertainment to those of a perverse turn of mind.

Probably, the last Christmas when the gates were closed was 1964, for the last Station Master was made redundant in the following June. The road was taken over by Avon County Council and the best evidence indicates that it was adopted by the County on 13th December 1972.

---

[1]*Bath Weekly Chronicle 28th November 1931*

Work in progress to lengthen the Keynsham & Somerdale platforms c1932. *Cadbury Ltd*

Avon Road (now Avon Mill `Lane) gates closed to traffic on Christmas Day 1962. *Author*

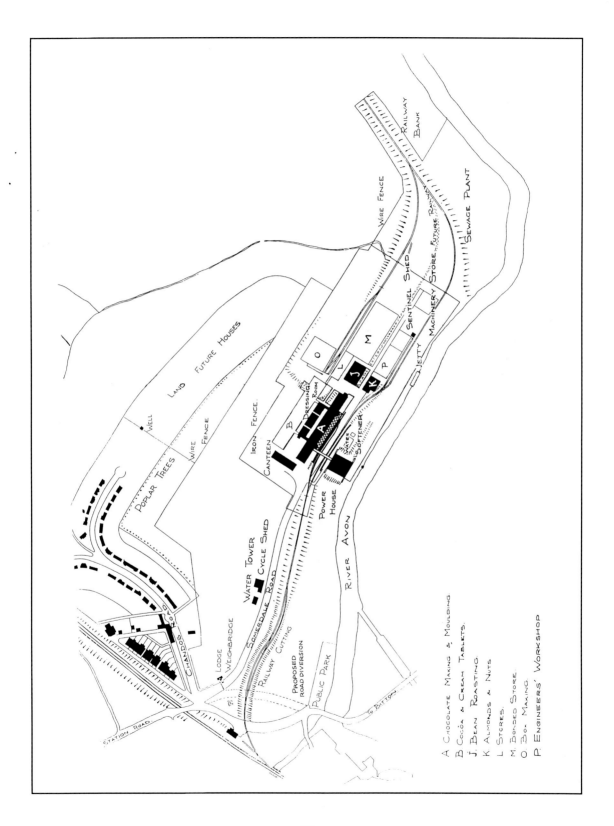

RAILWAY

BANK

SEWAGE PLANT

FUTURE RAILWAY

WIRE FENCE

SENTINEL SHED

MACHINERY STORE

JETTY

LAND FUTURE HOUSES

WELL

POPLAR TREES

IRON FENCE.

CANTEEN

WIRE FENCE

O

V

M

J

K

P

B

DRESSING ROOM

A

WATER SOFTENER

POWER HOUSE

WATER TOWER

CYCLE SHED

SOMERSDALE ROAD

RIVER AVON

RAILWAY CUTTING

WEIGHBRIDGE

LODGE

CHANDOS

PROPOSED ROAD DIVERSION

PUBLIC PARK

To BRITTON

STATION ROAD

A Chocolate Making & Moulding
B Cocoa & Cream Tablets.
J. Bean Roasting
K Almonds & Nuts
L Stores.
M. Bonded Store
O. Box Making.
P. Engineers' Workshop

79

8. The Fry's Workers' Trains

In this chapter there are references to railway jargon, locomotive and rolling stock movements, purposely inserted for historical completeness and for the benefit of railway historians.

During the 1920s when the chocolate firm of Fry's moved from their cramped premises in the Union Street area of central Bristol and built the new factory on a green field site on The Hams on the North West outskirts of Keynsham they called their factory 'Somerdale'. In consequence, the railway renamed their station Keynsham and Somerdale, with effect from 1st February 1925.

With an influx of 4,000 employees from Bristol, most of whom would have travelled by train, the GWR laid on additional trains specifically for the new traffic. By reference to a 1934 timetable, a number of trains can be identified as catering almost exclusively for Fry's passenger traffic. There were arrivals at:

    7.27am from Parson Street
    7.32am from Horfield
    8.36am from Clifton Down
    1.15pm from Severn Beach.

The first went forward to Westbury and the other three terminated at Keynsham. A quarter of a century later those four trains were still running at almost identical times. The 8.36am arrival was for the benefit of staff workers and the 1.15pm for the benefit of afternoon shift workers. All the trains ran on six days of the week, except that the 1.15pm was diverted to Temple Meads on Saturdays. The 7.27am from Parson Street called at Temple Meads, but the others traversed the curve between Dr Days Bridge Junction and North Somerset Junction thus avoiding Temple Meads. They all called at St Anne's Park.

Before the war there was Saturday morning working and that is reflected in the pattern of the return trains, later in the day. They were:

    Mondays to Fridays
        2.12pm to Stapleton Road (used
            by the early turn shift workers)
        5.32pm to Clifton Down
        5.36pm to North Filton Platform
        5.44pm to Parson Street

Saturdays only:
    12.12pm to Filton Junction
    12.17pm to Parson Street
    12.45pm to Clifton Down

Presumably, the office staff finished half an hour later than the factory on Saturdays.

The trains tell us something about the social status of the employees at the time of the removal of the factory from Bristol to Keynsham. The Parson Street train was well patronised because it served the densely populated areas of Bristol around Temple Meads, Bedminster and Parson Street itself. Much of the housing has long since vanished, either demolished by Hitler's bombs or by subsequent Local Authority clearance. Parson Street was also a most convenient point at which to commence or terminate trains, being adjacent to the Malago Vale carriage sidings which survived until the late 1980s

The train from Horfield served Ashley Hill, Stapleton Road and another clearance area at Lawrence Hill. The staff train started out from Clifton Down and first of all called at Redland and Montpelier, far more salubrious areas as befitted ladies and gentlemen of staff status. Sadly, they had to muck in with the workers on the way home.

At Keynsham, the route taken by employees to and from the station was across Station Hill and by the footpath alongside the siding; by far the shortest route. So, morning and evening, two male employees in their white dustcoats and distinctive white headdress were to be seen in the middle of Station Hill holding up the road traffic whilst the crowds crossed the road in safety. Tickets were, of course always checked by the porter on the gate.

During the 1950s, when the traffic was still at its peak, the author sometimes travelled on the 5.8pm from Bath to Bristol, the train being formed of six non-corridor coaches each seating five a side in ten compartments, ie 100 passengers per coach, except that the guards van coach only seated 60.

The train came into Bath empty, immediately following the 4.7pm from Swindon which departed from Bath at 4.57pm. So, there

Fry's employees arriving Keynsham and Somerdale on the 6.30am from Avonmouth Dock via Henbury on 11th June 1963. The engine, 5908 *Moreton Hall* was withdrawn from service a few weeks later.

Author

Ivatt 2–6–2T on the 5.15pm (FSX) to Henbury near Lodge Farm on 17th August 1961.   *Author*

were only a handful of passengers on board come 5.8pm, mostly travelling in true British solitary style in compartments meant for ten. One or two might join the train at Oldfield Park, but, more often than not, there would be no one to join or leave at Saltford. At the approach to Keynsham the train was usually brought to a stand awaiting the departure of the 5.25pm to Henbury which could be clearly seen still at the platform awaiting time. Looking out of the window it was possible to watch the 5.25pm depart and the signals set without delay for us to approach the station platform. The 5.25pm started from Keynsham, the empty stock having been bought out from Bristol.

Our train drew up at the still tightly packed platform, one drew a deep breath and waited for the worst. The door opened, a gaggle of giggling gregarious girls rapidly fell into the compartment which happened to stop opposite to where they were standing and fill the nine available empty seats. The doors slammed closed with a quick staccato like machine gun fire, the guard blew his whistle and another load of Fry's Angels[1] were on their way home, prompt at 5.28pm - just three minutes after the departure of the previous train. The gossip and the laughter was non-stop, for the Angels were predominately girls in the younger age brackets who were relieving themselves of the boredom of putting squiggles on chocolates, or whatever, for hours on end during the day.

No special arrangements were made for the few employees residing in the Bath direction, those employees used the normal timetabled trains which were at generally convenient times.

Having just read a brief resume of the Fry's workers' trains, we will now look at the early post war position in more detail, and follow that with the changes in the services that subsequently took place, leading up to their ultimate demise. However, first of all, some clarification of the railway geography may be useful to avoid confusion to the reader relating to the Severn Beach line. To some extent, the Severn Beach line was used by the railway to provide what, in effect, were circular services. Trains travelled out from Bristol via Clifton Down and Avonmouth and returned either from St Andrew's Road via Henbury, or from Severn Beach via Pilning Low Level. The Henbury line no longer has a passenger service and the Pilning Low Level line has been lifted. Some of the Fry's trains used the Henbury line, serving Henbury and North Filton Platform, and then on to the main line, calling at Filton (now replaced by Filton Abbey Wood), Horfield and Ashley Hill (both closed) before rejoining the Clifton Down line at Narrowways Junction just prior to Stapleton Road station. Some trains, of course, traversed the circle in the opposite direction.

During the early 1950s the workers' trains were as follows, and unless otherwise indicated, were formed of non-corridor stock.

1. 6.58am from Parson Street, with an arrival at Keynsham 7.23. The train continued to Bath where it formed the 8.00 back to Bristol. The regular motive power was a 55xx 2-6-2T or a pannier.
2. The 6.58am from North Filton Platform arrived at Keynsham at 7.27. Passengers from the Clifton Down line had a connection at Stapleton Road. The train continued to Westbury, calling at all stations and returned to Bristol with the stock as the 12.30pm from Westbury. The normal motive power was a large 2-6-2T of the 41XX, 51XX or 61XX classes.
3. The last morning train was the 7.43am (SX) from Avonmouth Dock, via Clifton Down, arriving at Keynsham at 8.26. That was the office workers' train with a connection at Stapleton Road off the Filton line. The train terminated at Keynsham, returning to Bristol as Empty Coaching Stock (ECS). Anything from a pannier to a Castle could be seen heading the train and, from time to time, engines from foreign sheds.
4. The 12.23pm (SX) from Severn Beach, which travelled via Clifton Down arrived at Keynsham at 1.10. That was the afternoon shift workers' train which formed the 2.15pm (SX) back to Stapleton Road for the off duty men. It was hauled by a large 2-6-2T. Passengers for Temple Meads travelled on the 1pm stopping

---

[1]*Fry's Angels was the generic term for the female employees both within the factory and by the railwaymen.*

service from Swindon which called a few minutes after the Stapleton Road train had left.

There was also a shift workers' train from Parson Street at 12.57 (SX) which called at Keynsham at 1.21pm en route to Bath. On Saturdays the train ran 15 minutes later, starting from Temple Meads instead of at Parson Street. A tank engine was used, anything from a pannier to a large 2-6-2T.

5. The first of the day shift homeward bound trains left Keynsham at 5.25pm (SX) for Henbury, with a connection at Stapleton Road for the Clifton Down line. A tank engine was provided, that having brought the ECS out from Bristol.

6. The second train left only three minutes later at 5.28pm. It was a timetabled train leaving Bath at 5.8pm. The ECS was brought out to Bath and the engine ran round the train at Bathampton. That was the train for Bedminster and Parson Street passengers. Motive power could be anything from a tank to a Castle, usually, but not invariably, provided from the Bath Road shed allocation. The tank/tender variation tended to go in cycles. In its final years it became the preserve of Hymek diesel hydraulics.

7. Night shift workers travelled to Keynsham on normal service trains. However, for homeward bound afternoon shift workers there was an unadvertised 10.14pm to Temple Meads. Normally, a GWR railcar was provided, but if that was not available it was a tank with a 'B' set[2]. An earlier part of the roster for the railcar was the 7.55pm from Bristol to Bath, returning from Bath at 9.8pm then ECS to Keynsham. It was while working the 9.8pm from Bath that the twin set railcars W35 and W36 caught fire and were burnt out at St Anne's Park. A couple of years earlier the rail car for the 10.14pm came to grief in Keynsham down loop. Instead of coming out on to the main line, it ran into the headshunt, demolishing the buffers and part of a masonry wall, finishing with 15 feet of its length overhanging a 20 foot drop into Avon Road. Fortunately there were no casualties. The road was closed until the debris could be removed.

The late 50s and early 60s was a period of continual change.

8. The afternoon shift train (12.23pm from Severn Beach) and the return 2.15pm to Stapleton Road was the first casualty. Patronage in both directions had been falling off badly. For those who were prepared to make the detour via Temple Meads, there were alternative timetabled trains within a few minutes of the discontinued services with connections into and out of the Severn Beach trains which had been diverted from Lawrence Hill to run into Temple Meads instead of travelling direct to Keynsham.

9. In June 1958, as an economy measure, there was a cut back in local Bristol services with the result that the fifteen to twenty who normally alighted at Keynsham off the 7.55pm from Temple Meads were forced to make alternative arrangements.

Within twelve months of the cut back, and following a substantial delivery of newly constructed diesel multiple units (DMUs), there resulted in a greatly enhanced local passenger service from 15th June 1959. Two changes were the result:

10. The 6.58am from North Filton Platform ceased to return from Westbury at 12.30pm. Instead it came back at 4.15pm (SX) from Westbury to become the 5.8pm from Bath and the 5.28pm from Keynsham. That eliminated one ECS working from Bristol.

11. The unadvertised 10.14pm from Keynsham was replaced by a timetabled service.

During 1960 Fry's introduced a 42 hour week which resulted in a slightly earlier finishing time on Mondays to Thursdays and very much earlier on Fridays. That had a number of repercussions.

---

[2]*A 'B' set was formed of two semi permanently coupled non-corridor suburban style coaches.*

Two Cl. 117 dmus in the Keynsham goods yard waiting to work the 4.10pm (Fridays only) Fry's workers' train to Avonmouth Dock via Henbury (right) and the 4.17pm (Fridays only) to Taunton on 13th April 1962.   *Author*

12. The 5.25pm (SX) to Henbury became the 5.15 (FSX)

13. The 5.28pm (SX) to Parson Street became the 5.20 (SX) which was the 4.15pm from Westbury with its departure from Bath advanced by six minutes.

14. An additional train was provided on Fridays at 4.5pm to Henbury.

15. Bristol bound passengers were catered tor by stopping the 1.40pm express from Paddington! That was a most unsatisfactory expedient, for the train was a poor timekeeper. Furthermore, the train was scheduled to stand at Temple Meads for twenty minutes and that would not please factory workers anxious to get home early on a Friday afternoon to Bedminster and Parson Street.

16. That arrangement only lasted until the September timetable; then passengers were catered for by altering the 4.35pm dmu from Temple Meads to Taunton to start from Keynsham at 4.17pm.

For the first time, special arrangements were made for the benefit of passengers travelling in the direction of Bath.

17. The 5pm from Temple Meads to Portsmouth & Southsea had unadvertised stops inserted at Keynsham and Oldfield Park (FSX)

18. There was at that time an ECS working from Bristol to Bath to form the 4.50pm to Swindon. On Fridays it was arranged for it to call at Keynsham at 4.7 then at Saltford and Oldfield Park. It only appeared in the public timetable from June to September 1961.

During the currency of the 1960 summer service two significant changes took place in engine rosters. St Philip's Marsh shed took over responsibility for the 6.57am from North Filton Platform together with the corresponding return working, using tender engines instead of tanks. Later it became the preserve of Hymek diesels. Secondly, the 5.15pm from Keynsham was taken over by Barrow Road engines, sometimes Ivatt tanks or Standard 4-6-0s of the 75xxx series. On at least one occasion the engine was a Stanier Black Five. The changes were occasioned by the closure of the Bath Road shed for redevelopment in connection with the forthcoming dieselisation of motive power.

The next batch of alterations came with the introduction of the winter service on 11th September 1961.

19. The 6.58am from Parson Street was incorporated into a new 6.30am restaurant car express from Weston-super-Mare to Paddington which called at Parson Street and Bedminster at the same time as the lately departed 6.58. That permitted Fry's passengers to stay longer in bed (if they so desired), for they now had 27 minutes on the train to have breakfast in the restaurant car (if they so desired) before they arrived at Keynsham.

20. The morning office workers' train was cut back to terminate at Lawrence Hill because it got in the way of a reorganised departure schedule of trains from Temple Meads in consequence of the introduction of the Bristol Pullman which departed at 8.15am. Although the train was hauled by 2-6-2T 4129 on its last day, it did have the distinction of being worked regularly by one of the first two diesel Hymeks put into traffic by BR. The other Hymek worked the 8.10am from Bristol to Portsmouth & Southsea, so there was the novelty of being able to see both at Keynsham within the space of ten minutes. The office workers' train regularly brought 30 to 40 passengers to Keynsham and its demise was not so much from lack of patronage, but because of its inconvenience in the new timetable. Those passengers were expendable. Until the Bristol Pullman, it fitted in quite comfortably between the 8.10 and 8.30am from Temple Meads. Now the 8.10 was retired to 8.18am (sometimes only on paper), there was insufficient time to fit in an 8.34am arrival at Keynsham - or so they said.

21. Because of the loss of the foregoing train, an unadvertised stop was inserted into the 8am Bristol to Weymouth, calling at 8.8am.

On 5th March 1962, the local services radiating from Bristol were severely pruned because the high hopes of improved patronage expressed back in 1959 failed to materialise. The results were:

22. The 11.52am from Chippenham to Temple Meads, used by a handful of women part time workers, ceased to run. It called at Keynsham around 12.40pm, but had varied by a few minutes either side over the years. The replacement was the 9.33am from Portsmouth & Southsea which had a stop inserted at 12.55pm (SX), but it took the women to Stapleton Road instead of Temple Meads. The women obviously did not want to go to Stapleton Road, so the train ceased to call at Keynsham in the following September.

23. The time hallowed 5.8pm from Bath to Parson Street, which had been advanced to 5.2 (see 10 and 13 above) was further advanced to 4.57pm to become the 5.15 from Keynsham and diverted to Henbury, thus eliminating the last ECS working out of Bristol.

24. There was no replacement for the 5.15pm to Parson Street. Passengers had to wait for the 4.37 from Chippenham which called at 5.23, but only called at St Anne's Park before terminating at Temple Meads. (A report in the *Railway Observer* during 1970 stated that the 4.48pm from Chippenham picked up eight to ten passengers at Keynsham - a far cry from ten years previous. The train itself was a single diesel unit, known among the railway fraternity as a "Bubble Car".)

25. Not surprisingly, the 6.30am restaurant car express from Weston-super-Mare ceased to call at Keynsham with the commencement of the 1962 winter service. By that time the number alighting at Keynsham could be counted on the fingers of one hand.

26. Following the closure of many Bristol local stations in 1964, including Henbury, Horfield and Ashley Hill, the two remaining trains (Nos 2 and 23) were diverted to run to and from Severn Beach via Clifton Down.

27. By the time of the 1974 May timetable the two remaining trains (both dmus) for Fry's workers could still be identified. There was a 6.17am from Severn Beach via Clifton Down, terminating at Keynsham at 7.21. The significant difference was that it was routed via

Temple Meads and stood there from 6.56 until 7.14. That was hardly an encouragement for early morning shift workers. There was still a 4.30pm from Westbury, calling at Keynsham at 5.16. That too sat at Temple Meads, but only for six minutes. A further pruning of the train service in 1979 saw the disappearance of the 4.30pm from Westbury. The 7.21am morning arrival had already disappeared. There the story ends.

The run down and final demise of the trains for Fry's employees was a gradual process, mainly as a result of factors outside the control of the railway. The traffic actually discarded was marginal for, in general, trains were not taken off until reduced patronage made the service uneconomic. Why did the patronage fall off? Here are some suggested reasons:

A. The shift of the population out of Bristol. A considerable acreage of Bedminster, and that surrounding Lawrence Hill, were housing clearance areas, resulting in an overspill into surrounding districts, one of which was Keynsham. During the ten years from 1951 to 1961 the population of Keynsham actually doubled from 6,000 to 12,000. During that decade the old Keynsham Urban District Council allocated several hundred houses to Bristol overspill. No doubt, many Fry's employees took the opportunity to live nearer their place of employment. To-day, a significant proportion of employees actually live in Keynsham.

B. As the older generation of the 1920s and 1930s became depleted through natural wastage their replacements were recruited from a wider catchment area, areas almost inevitably without any railway facilities. The coaches and buses took over, but now in 1996 their patronage is so thin that it is probably only a matter of time before they disappear like the trains.

C. A glimpse at Fry's car park from the passing train tells its own story.

D. Modern technology has taken its toll. There were some 4,000 employees who migrated from Bristol in the 1920s, a figure which remained reasonably constant for many years. By September 1987 the number of employees was down to 1,350 and is expected to fall further and to ultimately level off around 850, and without loss of production.

So if this chapter can be construed as an inquest into the death of a railway service, the verdict can be no other than death from natural causes.

The railway recognised that the traffic had gone for good when the station name reverted to plain Keynsham on 6th May 1974. Fifteen years later, one gentleman could still be heard over the public address system at Temple Meads announcing trains to call at Keynsham and Somerdale. Somebody should have told him!

9. Excursions to Somerdale

During the 1930s, and again after the war, a popular train outing was to visit Fry's chocolate factory at Somerdale. Special trains were run from many parts of the country direct to Keynsham and Somerdale station which is situated almost outside the main factory gates. The blurb on the railway handbills which advertised the excursions varied in detail, but the following is a good example:

"After a tour of the factory, every visitor receives a dainty tea, together with a generous size box of freshly made chocolates. This is followed by a twenty mile drive through charming Somerset countryside to the Avon Gorge, which is spanned by the famous Clifton Suspension Bridge. The final run through the old world City of Bristol with its towering University, its Cathedral and the slender tapering spire of St Mary Redcliffe leaves a lasting impression of a memorable day."

Another version read "...... including a conducted tour of Messrs J.S. Fry and Sons' Works and Garden Village". (Presumably Chandos Road!).

"Bristol" motor coaches were provided for the tour of Bristol, a concern then known as the Bristol Tramways and Carriage Co Ltd, predecessors of the Bristol Omnibus Company, which in turn, since deregulation, has been, divided up into a number of separate entities, of which City Line and Badgerline operate within the Bristol area.

All return train journeys commenced from the Bristol Temple Meads station, often two or more hours after completion of the road tour. The only restriction for visitors was that children under the age of ten were not permitted in the factory.

The Bristol Divisional Superintendent of the GWR in his annual report to the Superintendent of the Line at Paddington made first mention of "Educational Excursions" to Somerdale in his report for 1929. It was in that year that the railway tested the temperature with the running of twelve trains to Keynsham and Somerdale from unspecified originating points. For the next four years (1930-33) detailed lists of originating stations were given, together with the number of passengers carried. Thereafter, the lists of originating stations were omitted. It was good business, for in the ten years to 1938 a quarter of a million passengers .were carried, of whom approximately 90% participated in the factory tour. The other 25,000 passengers took the opportunity to visit relatives, or just see the sights of Bristol. (It is known that some keen train spotters of the day from Plymouth got no further than the end of the platform at Temple Meads!)

Passengers on the trains off the LMS system were all carried through to Keynsham and Somerdale. The probable explanation is because their trains approached Bristol via the GWR route from Yate and therefore would not stop to set down passengers at a GWR station in Bristol such as Stapleton Road.

A number of excursions were organised by schools and by local and national newspapers. In October 1930 six trains, running on six different days, each purporting to carry 500 passengers were organised by an unspecified local newspaper.

	Number of trains run	Number of passengers	Number on factory visit
1929	12	6628	*
1930	41	19408	17393
1931	44	18255	16560
1932	58	21016	18482
1933	68	25875	23484
1934	88	36800	*
1935	95	34849	*
1936	111	37126	*
1937	113	35380	*
1938	79	25394	*
Total	709	260731	

* Not specified

Analysis of Trains by originating railway

	GWR	LMS	LNER	SR	Total
1930	29	7	-	5	41
1931	21	14	-	9	44
1932	21	20	2	15	58
1933	27	18	-	23	68

The range of stations from which through bookings could be made is intriguing. As an example, there was a train starting from Cornwood, a village of no significance in South Devon, picking up at intermediate stations to Norton Fitzwarren, where a connection was made for passengers from Barnstaple and all the small stations on that branch line. The train would have started from Plymouth and run empty to Cornwood, and it did not call at Taunton after Norton Fitzwarren. The larger centres of population were provided for by other excursions on other days.

From the handbills we learn:
1. The fine tuning of child fares to the nearest halfpenny.

2. The fact that lunch and supper were available on some of the trains and the variation in the charges levied.

GWR Lunch 2/9 or 3/4. Supper 2/9 or 3/4. (Total 5/6 or 6/8) [27p or 33p].

LMS Lunch and supper inclusive, including gratuities, 5/6 [27p]

SR Lunch 2/6 Supper 2/6 (Total 5/-) [25p]

Tea time in the Somerdale Visitors' Dining Room. All the ladies wore hats, but few of the visitors smiled.   *Cadbury Ltd*

Centre spread from the visitors' guide book showing the general factory layout.   *Cadbury Ltd*

3. In some cases there was an arrangement for Corporation buses to meet trains which arrived back at their destinations in the small hours. In pre-war days that was by no means an unusual arrangement. The bus conductor would establish the various destinations for his passengers and, together with the driver, arrange a convenient route of travel with a complete disregard for conventional day time bus routes. The fare scale of 6d (2½p) adult and 3d (1p) child was generally uniform throughout the country. It needs to be remembered that Corporation transport was usually restricted to within the appropriate Local Authority boundary and that urban sprawl was not so extensive as it is to-day. The night fare quoted would be at least double, and probably treble, the normal day time fare for the distance travelled.

In addition to the public excursions, trade visits were organised from various parts of the country, all by special train. At least five such visits were arranged during the summer of 1939, although due to the outbreak of war, the last two were almost certainly cancelled. These were highly organised affairs and the trade visitors were allowed one guest each. On the outward journey a whist drive was arranged, a pack of playing cards and a score card at each table. Playing cards and score cards were collected towards the end of the journey, with the score cards placed in a sealed envelope. The prize winners were announced during the afternoon. Lunch was served on the train as guests of Fry's, together with soft drinks, tea and coffee.

Prior to making a tour of the factory, guests were segregated according to the value of their accounts. Following the tour, afternoon tea was served to the guests in the visitors' tea room and the "standard 9d (4p) tea" was provided, consisting of:

Brown and white bread and butter
Sandwiches
Assorted cakes
Crunchie and Tiffin
Tea or cocoa

"Guides will hand around cigarettes in special wooden boxes"

It will be observed that coffee was not available at teatime.

The day concluded with everyone being taken on the standard road tour of Bristol and its environs. Supper was available on the return train journey, but it would appear that guests had to pay for that themselves. Playing cards were also available upon request and the stewards were instructed to collect up as many packs as possible before journey end!

The Manchester Trade Visit was on 5th July, starting from the Mayfield Station at 8.40am, getting back at 1.47am the next morning, for which the fare was 16/3 (81p). The train called at principal stations to Walsall via the Potteries. Walsall departure was at 10.53am, back at 11.26pm for a fare 11/- (55p). The train capacity was 500 and the estimated number of participants was 430.

Similar trains were scheduled to run as follows:
6th July from Nottingham, Loughborough Leicester, Rugby and Coventry and intermediate stations. Train capacity 500.
12th July from Banbury, Oxford, Reading and intermediate stations. Train capacity 350. Acceptances 332.
20th September from Colchester, Cambridge, Leighton Buzzard and intermediate stations.
21st September from Ramsgate, Margate etc.

From some stations guests had to travel by ordinary train as a connecting service for the first portion of journey.

As there would not have been time to serve 332 lunches on the train from Banbury/Oxford/Reading on 12th July, lunch was taken in Fry's dining hall. Catering was done by the New County Hotel, Gloucester.

Strictly outside the preview of the Railway at Keynsham, but by way of contrast, Shamrock and Rambler ran a road tour starting from Holderness Road, Bournemouth every Tuesday and Thursday during the season. A free taxi from home to Holderness Road was provided. The length of journey precluded a stop at Salisbury, but there was two hours at Bristol on The Downs, with time to visit the Zoo. A combined admittance ticket to the Zoo together with a four course lunch was recommended for the inclusive price of 2/9 (14p). (Admittance only in 1994 was £5.50!). After lunch the tour continued, taking the Bath Road, turning off at the village of Keynsham in order to visit the chocolate factory at Somerdale. The fare for that outing was 10/6 (52½p) compared with 6/9 (34p) by rail on 29th August, approximately two thirds of the coach fare.

That being the only handbill for coach travel found in the file at Bournville, it may be presumed that the railway had virtually a monopoly in the days prior to the war.

In addition to the special trains, a thousand or more passengers from local stations with excursion tickets travelled to Keynsham and Somerdale each year on ordinary timetabled trains, but the total figures were not always reported. One of the most extraordinary of such bookings offered was from Malmesbury. Passengers left Malmesbury at 12.15 but did not arrive at Keynsham & Somerdale until 2.18, having taken two hours for a 41 mile journey. There were three changes of train in the first 21 miles to Chippenham, that being only about ten miles as the crow flies from the starting point. Changes of train were at Little Somerford, Wootton Bassett and Chippenham. Excursionists joining the train at Little Somerford had to remember to ask the guard to stop at Wootton Bassett as that was a request stop only! Having eventually arrived at Chippenham they joined a train which originated at Swindon, but did not stop at Wootton Bassett, but then called at all stations and halts to Keynsham and Somerdale.

1939 poster.

SUMMARY OF EDUCATIONAL EXCURSIONS TO KEYNSHAM AND SOMERDALE
1933

GWR Trips		On Tour	On Train
24th March 1933	Hayes & Harlington (Schools)	587	587
5th April	Plymouth & Exeter	342	583
6th	Rhondda Valley	286	286
27th	Swansea	510	510
2nd May	Weymouth, Swindon etc	544	544
4th	Aberdare (Aberdare Leader)	500	500
12th	Milford Haven	160	179
15th	Birmingham (Birmingham Gazette)	510	510
17th	Llynfi and Ogmore Valleys & Cardiff	500	500
22nd	Penzance (Schools)	546	546
23rd	Penzance (Schools)	624	624
29th	Paddington (Daily Sketch)	492	492
12th June	Paddington	248	393
14th	Cardiff (Western Mail)	522	614
15th	Worcester etc	381	408
21st	Barnstaple	497	511
22nd	Llanelly	564	564
29th	Eastern Valley	321	321
5th July	Plymouth & Exeter	595	700
11th	Banbury	320	350
18th	Plymouth	500	500
17th August	Cheltenham Spa	128	133
13th September	Western Valleys	523	523
14th	Plymouth. & Exeter	502	747
15th	Penzance (Schools)	618	618
26th	Cardiff	555	555
12th October	Rhondda Valley	500	500
		12375	13298

LM&S Trips		On Tour	On Train
8th May	Matlock	296	296
11th	Nottingham	157	157
18th	Redditch	299	299
25th	Northampton	164	164
7th June	Chesterfield	246	246

LM&S Trips		On Tour	On Train
8th	Birkenhead	119	119
20th	Bletchley	439	439
26th	Kettering	131	131
27th	Northampton	378	378
6th July	Sheffield	325	325
10th	Cambridge	326	326
20th	Wolverhampton	417	417
25th	Southport	121	121
23rd August	Bromsgrove	121	121
24th	Sheffield	181	181
29th	Nottingham	144	144
31st	Coventry	290	290
7th September	Liverpool	422	422
		4576	**4576**

Southern Company's Trips		On Tour	On Train
25th April	Portsmouth & Southsea (Schools)	486	486
26th	Portsmouth & Southsea (Schools)	310	354
3rd May	Brighton	172	226
10th	Worthing	185	223
24th	Torrington (2 trains)	684	693
8th June	Twickenham	65	96
28th	Christchurch	418	507
4th July	Portsmouth & Southsea	521	643
12th	Gillingham (? Dorset or Kent)	228	267
13th	Brighton (2 trains)	413	522
19th	Clapham Junction	115	180
16th August	Winchester	409	454
30th	Norwood Junction	356	440
6th September	Christchurch	354	477
20th	Portsmouth & Southsea (2 trains)	601	930
27th	Deal	109	133
28th	Brighton	298	382
4th October	Worthing	324	398
5th	Ramsgate	223	263
11th	Winchester	262	327
		6533	**8001**

"Educational Excursions" and "Trips" are in the railway terminology of the day.

Total number of passengers 25,875

PRO Rail 235/553

10. Fry's Show Train

Today, show trains on the railway are an accepted form of advertisement, whether it be for trade products or for service industries, such as tourism. Back in 1933, when Fry's put their Show Train on the railroad it was described as "A novel development in British salesmanship". The inauguration of the train was considered to be of sufficient importance as to warrant an official luncheon at Somerdale on 30th May 1933, when the principal guest, Viscount Weymouth, (the local MP,) was billed to launch the project. Other distinguished guests included:

Mr Thomas Wise	Lord Mayor of Bristol
Mr A. Maynard	GWR Chief Goods Manager
Mr F.R. Potter	Principal Assistant to the Superintendent of the Line
Mr G.R. Pole	GWR Bristol Divisional Superintendent

MENU

Grape Fruit au Marasquin
-
Consomme Brunoise
-
Salmon Mayonnaise
-

Roast Fore Quarter of Lamb - Mint Sauce
Roast Chicken York Ham
Roast Sirloin of Beef
-

Dressed Salads

New Potatoes
-

Strawberry Iced Souffle
-
Cheese Butter Biscuits
-
Coffee

The train was made up with three coaches which had been converted, one from a restaurant car which was positioned between two former scenery vans. (Scenery vans were for the use of travelling theatrical companies). One van was fitted out to its entire length for the trade display in twelve three tiered show cases displaying over 200 of Fry's products.

The former restaurant car became a tea lounge "tastefully decorated with Lloyd Loom furniture, comprising eight tables and twenty chairs". All the panelling was in mahogany. The coach also contained sleeping quarters for the two salesmen who accompanied the train as it toured the country. The third coach housed the electrical plant which provided the necessary internal illumination.

On the exterior, "Fry's Show Train" was boldly lettered in gold (in relief) on a royal blue background.

The first visit of the train to London for the benefit of the general public was from Monday 25th November 1935 until Saturday 30th. The venue, of course, was Paddington station. Admission charges were 2d for adults and 1d for children. The whole proceeds were donated to St Mary's Hospital, Paddington. A free sample chocolate bar was given to every visitor to the value of the admission money.

The train toured most of the country each year, being stabled for exhibition purposes in convenient station bay platforms or in adjacent sidings. It was attached to passenger trains when on the move from point to point. The annual reports from the Bristol Divisional Superintendent to the Superintendent of the Line make no mention of the train visiting Scotland. All four railways co-operated in the venture and the report for 1938 may be taken as typical.

"The Spring tour commenced at Newport on 3rd January. The train then visited various stations in South Wales, Wolverhampton, Shrewsbury, Wrexham and Liverpool. It then proceeded to the LM&S Company's system, returning to Gloucester for exhibition on 22nd March, then to Keynsham and Somerdale. On

9th May the train was on show at Wells, Bridgwater and various stations in the West of England until 26th May, when it passed to the Southern Railway's system at Exeter, thence to L&NE and L&MS Companys, returning to Liverpool (Lime Street) on 13th October.

The train returned to Keynsham and Somerdale on 5th November after a tour of Midlands and South Wales".

TAILPIECE Fry's "novel development in British salesmanship" was quickly taken up by His Master's Voice (The Gramophone Co.), who had their own show train of converted GWR vehicles running in 1934.

A more complete account of Fry's Show Train appears in the Great Western Railway magazine for July 1933.

11. Four Industrial Sidings

To The East of Keynsham station there were four private sidings, two installed during the inter war period and two after the end of the Second World War. On the up side there was, the important Fry's siding, to which a whole chapter has been devoted. Just a little further East the well known firm of E.S.&A. Robinson had their paper mill, opened in 1932. On the same site there was a small affiliated concern trading as Paper Sacks Ltd who had a short siding terminating at a loading platform. The siding was first used in May 1929, but Paper Sacks Ltd vacated the site in 1930, moving to Northfleet in Kent where the well known concern, Blue Circle, operated the then largest cement works in the country. That was a logical move as a significant proportion of the output was in the shape of paper sacks for cement. The conveyor from their building to the loading platform was still in situ in 1990. After the departure of Paper Sacks Ltd, the only known use of the loading platform was for the despatch of munitions during the Second World War. The edifice was demolished around about the time that the siding was lifted in 1969.

By the time the paper mill was opened, the siding had been extended to the factory gate in Unity Road. A run round loop was provided, together with a short branch towards the rear of the mill. The siding was used for the delivery of pulp and coal for the boilers. Finished rolls of paper were despatched by rail until the 1950s when British Road Services took over. Coal delivery ceased during the early 1960s when the boilers were converted to oil. In latter days the siding was shunted, as required, around 8 o'clock in the morning. In 1969 came Multiple Aspect Signalling (MAS), controlled from the new power signal box at Temple Meads. In preparation, British Rail wanted to be rid of as much pointwork as possible (track simplification they call it) and with that in view, they gave notice to Robinson's

The two Robinson paper mill shunters. The wreck in the foreground is Avonside 2013 of 1932 and, in the rear, the conventional four wheel Ruston, 23rd July 1966. *Author*

The Brown Boveri gas turbine 18000 (colloquially christened *Kerosene Castle*) on the 7.45am Bristol to Paddington at Pixash lane in October 1954. The Tate and Lyle siding can be seen on the left leading to a five bar gate and a footpath, neither of which are there now. *Author*

to lift the siding. On the other hand, Robinson's wished to retain the facilities, but British Rail would only agree provided a guaranteed number of trucks were conveyed to or from the siding each week. So, in October 1969 the siding was disconnected from the main line and the track removed as far as the warning board. The warning board left in situ informed engine drivers that "All trains must stop dead here."!

Robinson's had their own two small shunting locomotives. One was a conventional four wheel Ruston and Hornsby size 48, class DS 235519. Sometime after the siding fell into disuse it was given a cosmetic coat of paint and languished in situ until moved to the preservation site at nearby Bitton on 26th January 1974. Four months later, on 27th May, during one of Bitton's Open Days, it was pressed into passenger service following the failure of the steam locomotive. The grunts

and groanings will be a never forgotten memory as the machine made its way at walking pace towing just one brake van with its human cargo.

The second locomotive on the paper mill site was a four wheel Avonside works number 2013 of 1932. (The Avonside Engine Co Ltd, of Kingswood, Bristol, was essentially a steam locomotive builder which closed in 1935). That locomotive was a two speed machine with a four cylinder paraffin engine which was started on petrol. Speeds were 3.1 or 6mph! In its later days it sported a Hunslet radiator grill. When photographed in 1966 it was little more than a wreck, although it was really a historic piece of machinery, one of three built by the firm in 1932. The other two were constructed as broad gauge, one going to Australia and the other to India. Unfortunately the Keynsham machine was broken up and the subsequent history of the other two is unknown.[1]

[1] *The British Internal Combustion Locomotive 1894-1940 Brian Webb (David & Charles 1973)*

Class 14 D9521 shunting the Square Grip Reinforcement Co's siding at 06.45 on 23rd June 1966.

Author

The other two private sidings were on the down side. The earlier of the two was into the Tate and Lyle depot which was adjacent to Pixash Lane. The siding had capacity for only two or three wagons and had a very short life from 1952 until 1966. It did not see a great deal of use and the author never saw anything in there.

The fourth siding was a little nearer to Keynsham serving The Square Grip Reinforcement Co (London) Ltd whose premises were situated on the Ashmead Industrial Estate. The siding had an even shorter lifespan (from 1955 until 1966 when the firm moved to Yate), but unlike Tate and Lyle, there were regular deliveries of steel bars into the siding. Delivery was effected early in the morning, around 6.30am because it entailed occupation of the down main line for the best part of half an hour. The performance, although a routine railway operation, was in the layman's eyes quite involved. The shunter who accompanied the train from the goods yard had first to obtain telephonic permission from the signalman in the East Signal Box

who then electrically unlocked a key in the lineside cabinet. That key permitted the shunter to operate the points that led from the main line into the siding. The sequence of events was then:

1. The locomotive which had already propelled from the goods yard the two loaded wagons along the down line in the up direction, propelled the wagons into the siding.
2. The two empty wagons already in the siding were attached to the two loaded ones, and all four removed from the siding, the two empty one being parked on the main line.
3. The two loaded ones were drawn forward and then propelled into the siding and left there.
4. The locomotive coupled up to the two empties parked on the main line and returned to the goods yard, the shunter having returned the points key to the lineside cabinet the signalman electrically locked it away

The western approach to Saltford tunnel from Brunel's Tunnel House Hotel. A Cl.47 approaches on 22nd September 1987. *Author*

Pixash Lane bridge, the only point of access to the Broadmead Industrial Estate for HGVs and other wide or high vehicles. Schweppes was formerly Tate and Lyle

Author

12. Excursions from Keynsham

On 5th July 1841, Mr Thomas Cook organised the first ever railway excursion, which ran from Leicester to Loughborough, a distance of 12½ miles. Cook's enterprise soon took off, for McDermott records that on Michaelmas Day 1842 between 600 and 700 persons from Bristol, Bath, Chippenham and Swindon were conveyed at half the usual fare for a day in the Metropolis. He also records a return excursion from the Great Exhibition at the Crystal Palace which came to grief just short of the Brislington tunnel on 10th August 1851.

The first mention of Keynsham that has been discovered was in 1857, in an advertisement which was displayed in the Bristol Mirror and General Advertiser. Every Wednesday during July of that year there was an excursion from Bristol, Bath and Bradford -on-Avon to Weymouth. A footnote added that "Parties of not less than eight, upon giving notice to the Superintendent at Bristol, can be taken up or set down at Limpley Stoke or Freshford." Perhaps representations were made to the Superintendent at Bristol because for Wednesdays in August the footnote included Keynsham as well as Limpley Stoke and Freshford.[1]

The morning train left Bristol at 7.30am and the return service from Weymouth was at 5.15pm. The return fare from Bristol was 7/- (35p) first class and 5/- (25p) in a covered carriage. A fare from Keynsham was not quoted.

A random search of 19th Century Bristol newspapers reveals a generally negative approach to excursion facilities at Keynsham, yet bookings were often available from much smaller communities along the line of route. For example, on August Bank Holiday Monday 1882, there were excursion bookings to Weymouth from most stations between Bristol (at 6am) and Yeovil, including Limpley Stoke, Witham and Sparkford.

From Bristol at 6.30am on the same day, there was an excursion to London (including bookings to Crystal Palace) with pick ups at the small stations at Box and Wootton Bassett, but not Keynsham. Very early starts seem to indicate that excursionists had to be got out of the way before respectable travellers were about.

On 3rd, 4th and 5th of August that same year, Australia were playing Gloucestershire at cricket at Clifton, which at that time was still a part of Gloucestershire. Cheap fares to Clifton Down station, at single fare plus a quarter return, were available by certain unspecified trains from Swindon, Taunton, Wells and Westbury and intermediate stations. Keynsham supporters, presumably, were able to take advantage on the trains from Swindon and Westbury.

On Wednesday, 24th January 1906, there was a half day excursion from Warminster to Bristol, picking up at Keynsham at 4.9pm or 5.15pm, when the fare from Keynsham was given as 6d (2½p) return. Children under 12 travelled at half fare. No luggage was allowed and the return train from Temple Meads was at the late hour of 11.30pm. The attractions listed on the handbill were as follows:

Pantomime Mother Goose
  Princes Theatre, Park Row
Pantomime Goody Two Shoes
  Theatre Royal, King Street
Variety Entertainment
  People's Palace, Baldwin Street
Poole's Myriorama
and Variety Entertainment,
  Colston Great Hall
Bristol Art Gallery
  Queens Road   Admission Free
Bristol Museum
  Queens Road   Admission Free

A similar excursion was run on Wednesday, 14th February, except Poole's Myriorama was omitted. A myriorama was a magic lantern show with a picture composed of interchangeable slides which could be combined into a variety of pictures. One really has to see such a show to appreciate the wonder conveyed to Victorian and Edwardian audiences.

---

[1] *Saturday 1st August edition*

For the years 1909-14 and 1923-38 there are at the Public Record Office, Kew, extensive, maybe complete files of excursion handbills for the Bristol Division.[2] Handbills in those days were printed on low grade paper, each offer strung up with string and hung up slightly above eye level in a long untidy row beside the booking office window. Self selection they call it to-day. Late offers were cyclostyled on to foolscap sheets of duplicating paper with the date, destination timings and fare inserted in bold capitals and numerals on to the master by hand. Normal handbills were uniformly about six inches wide, but the length varied from about nine to eleven inches.

PRE 1914

In the days prior to the First World War there was quite a selection of regular excursion bookings available from a wide range of stations in North Somerset, and in North Wiltshire. Space precludes doing more than pick out a few examples of what was available from Keynsham and these have been selected from the programme for 1910. In many cases there were restrictions on the days for travel and the times when travel would be valid. That is not so different from what appertains to-day, both on British Rail and the long distance road coach network.

First, there was the "Saturday to Monday in London" ticket, which we would now call a week-end ticket. For 23/9 (£1-19) first class, and 12/- (60p) third class, through bookings were available, not only to Paddington, but also to the seventeen suburban stations as listed. Most of those stations still exist and those that do fall into two broad groups (a) stations on the Metropolitan line to Hammersmith, in which the GWR had a 50% interest and (b) stations on the line through what is now Kensington Olympia to Victoria, over which the GWR exercised running powers. A strange feature within the conditions of travel was that passengers could return by any train on Saturday or Monday, but only after 6am (sic) on Sunday. The stations listed on the handbill were as follows:

Acton	St Quentin Park & Wormwood Scrubs
Westbourne Park	Uxbridge Road
Royal Oak	Kensington Addison Road
Notting Hill & Ladbroke Grove	
	West Brompton
Latimer Road	Chelsea & Fulham
Wood Lane	Battersea
Shepherds Bush	Clapham Junction
Hammersmith	Victoria
	Liverpool Street (Metropolitan)

There were circular rail and coach tours through the Mendip Hills.

Tour 1. To Winscombe by rail, thence by char-a-banc or brake to Cheddar via Shipham, Charterhouse and Cheddar Gorge, returning by rail from Cheddar. Fare from Keynsham 6/- (30p) first class, 4/- (20p) third class

Tour 2. To Cheddar by rail, thence by char-a-banc or brake to Winscombe via Axbridge, Compton Bishop and Webbington, returning by rail from Winscombe Fare from Keynsham 5/3 (26p) first class, 3/3 (16p) third class.

For both tours the train departed from Keynsham at 10.49am or 1.11pm, but the 1.11pm on Saturdays was only for Tour 1.

The service between Winscombe and Cheddar was performed by Mr Alfred Weeks' "well horsed char-a-banc (or other suitable vehicles)". There was a charge of an extra shilling for a box seat, which had to be pre booked with at least two days notice. There was no first class accommodation on Mr Weeks' vehicles.

On Mondays and Thursdays only there were excursion facilities to Clevedon and Weston-super-Mare at 9.28am from Keynsham with a fare of 2/- (10p) to either destination. The return train was at 7.50pm from Weston Locking Road, or 8pm from Clevedon. On production of a GWR ticket, there was a reduced fare of six pence single or nine pence return between Weston and Clevedon on the

---

[2]*PRO reference Rail 253/567 forward*

Weston, Clevedon and Portishead Railway. At Weston-super-Mare "electric tramway cars run on weekdays between the Excursion Platform and the Grand Pier, Knightstone Pavilion, Burnbeck Pier, Sanatorium etc".

Similar facilities were available on Wednesdays at the same fare, but only on the 1.11pm for Clevedon, 2.2pm for Weston and 4.13pm to both destinations.

On Fridays and Saturdays there were week-end tickets to Weston-super-Mare, available on any train for 3/- (15p) first class or 2/6 (12½p) third class.

It would appear that Tuesdays and Sundays were full fare days.

During the summer months there were "long period" and "short period" excursions to South Devon and to Cornish stations with, for example, fares to Torquay at 7/6 (37½p) and 9/6 (47½p) respectively and to Plymouth at 9/- (45p) and 12/- (60p) third class only.

The rules for the return journey are worthy of a verbatim quote.

"Passengers going on Saturdays return as follows: Those holding "Short Period" tickets return on the following Monday, and those holding "Long Period" tickets return on the following Monday week. Those going on Monday return on the following Monday or Monday week. Passengers going on Monday or Saturday have the option of returning on the following Saturday or Saturday week if there is a train running."

The outward train was the 5.20am from Swindon which picked up at Keynsham at 6.55am and arrived at Plymouth nearly five hours later at 11.35am. Return from Plymouth was 12 noon on Mondays and 7.10pm on Saturdays.

An interesting one off was the Millenary of the Bishopric of Bath and Wells which was celebrated at Wells from 22nd to 26th June 1908. An excursion fare of 3/- (15p) return to Wells (change at Bristol Temple Meads) was available on the 8.35am departure from Keynsham on the 22nd only, the day of the visit of the Prince and Princess of Wales who in 1910 ascended the throne as King George V and Queen Mary. On the following day there were the Mothers Union celebrations with cheap tickets advertised from Twerton, but not from Keynsham.

THE INTER-WAR YEARS

In the inter-war period there was a wide range of excursions available from Keynsham, but again, space only permits a limited selection of the more interesting. Commencing in 1923, and operative for a number of years following, there were attractive excursion facilities by rail to Bath, then by launch on the Kennet and Avon Canal, returning by rail from either Bradford-on-Avon, Avoncliff or Limpley Stoke. The trip could be done in reverse, or out and back by launch, and was available from mid May until mid September. The handbill warned passengers that it was a 25 minute walk from Bath station to Darlington Wharf, a location which, presumably, is now known as Sydney Wharf.

Suitable trains from Keynsham were given as 8.44am, 9.58am, 11.12am, 1.35pm and 2.34pm

The launch timetable is as set out:

Bath	10.30	2.30	6.30	▲ 12.45	4.45	8.45
Bathampton	10.51	2.51	6.51	12.24	4.24	8.24
Dundas	11.39	3.39	7.39	11.36	3.36	7.36
Limpley Stoke	11.51	3.51	7.51	11.24	3.24	7.24
Avoncliff	12.22	4.22	8.22	10.53	2.53	6.53
Bradford-on-Avon	▼ 12.45	4.45	8.45	10.30	2.30	6.30

Great Western Railway.

Messrs. J. S. FRY & SONS
SPECIAL EXCURSIONS.

BRISTOL STATIONS to

LONDON

SATURDAY, JULY 5th.

AMENDED TIMES.

No. 1 Train

		a.m.
Clifton Down	dep.	5 5
Redland	,,	5 7
Montpelier	,,	5 10
Stapleton Road	,,	5 15
St Annes Park	,,	5 22
Keynsham	,,	5 30
Bath	,,	5 41
Wembley for Sudbury arr.		8 45

No. 1 Return Train will leave Willesden Jct. at 10.55 p.m.

No. 2 Train

		a.m.
Lawrence Hill	dep.	5 55
Stapleton Road	,,	6 2
Wembley for Sudbury arr.		9 10

No. 2 Return Train will leave Willesden Jct. at 11.10 p.m.

No. 3 Train

		a.m.
Bedminster	dep.	4 47
Temple Meads	,,	4 54
Wembley for Sudbury arr.		8 0

No. 3 Return Train will leave Willesden Jct. at 10.40 p.m.

Forward Journey. Passengers travel direct to Wembley for Sudbury Station.

Return Journey. Passengers proceed from Wembley for Sudbury Station to Willesden Junction in the evening by any train in sufficient time to join the Return Specials from Willesden Junction as above.

Trains run every few minutes between Wembley for Sudbury and Willesden Junction, the journey taking about six minutes, but ample time should be allowed in case of heavy traffic at this period.

BY ORDER.

Handbill for British Empire Exhibition excursion to Wembly, 1924.   *PRO Kew Rail 253/574*

The fares quoted were:

		Rail		Launch	Fare
Tour	1	To Bath	To	Bradford on Avon & return	3/2 (16p) adult
	2	Bradford-on-Avon		Bath (or vice versa)	3/-(15p)
	3	Avoncliff		Bath (”)	2/9 (14p)
	4	Limpley Stoke		Bath (”)	2/5 (12p)

The fares were four pence or five pence cheaper from Saltford.

All fares were increased by three pence in 1924.

For the 1923 season, from all stations within the programme, a total of 3617 tickets were issued and the revenue was £475.

Arrangements for the Cup Final were far different from these days of rampant hooliganism. It was a very long day, and it does not need much imagination to visualise the bleary eyed, travel worn , but happy band making their way home through the High Street in the small hours of Sunday morning. The excursion train left Taunton at 3am, picked up at Keynsham at 4.37am and arrived at Kensington Addison Road at 7.42am. In 1925, the match was between Cardiff City and Sheffield United and the fans had until 12 midnight to celebrate (or otherwise), before the return train left Paddington, setting down at Keynsham at the bewitching hour of 2.42am. The detailed timings varied by the odd minute or two over the years and by the latter half of the 30s the inward service was routed to Paddington instead of Addison Road

In pre-war days the railways regularly ran one off excursions to attractive destinations well beyond what could be achieved in half a day. On 25th April and 2nd May 1937 there were attractive excursions to Holland via Liverpool Street and The Hook. The programme included:

A coach tour of the bulbfields and The Hague
Lunch at Haarlem
Tea at Hotel Carlton, Amsterdam
Supper on the boat

All for £3.11s.0d. (£3-55) from Bristol, or £3.10s.0d. (£3-50) from Bath. No doubt, some of the more affluent members of the Keynsham community availed themselves of the opportunity.

Two years earlier, on 30th June 1935 there was an excursion to Cherbourg which actually called to pick up at Keynsham at 5.55am. The fare was 19/6) (97p). The boat sailed from Weymouth at 9am and was timed to arrive at Cherbourg at 1pm. British or Continental time was not specified, but the return sailing was at 6pm (English time). Arrival at Weymouth Quay was shown as 10.30pm and the train departure was advertised as "about 11pm," On the reverse of the handbill there was a somewhat indistinct map of Cherbourg - in French!

In contrast to those marathons of early starts and/or early finishes (next morning) there were the local football excursions. On 12th January 1935 there was Bristol City v Bury and Bristol Rovers v Manchester United. There was a special train from Westbury, calling at Keynsham at 1.40pm. To Temple Meads or Stapleton Road the return fare was 5d (2p), or to Ashton Gate by through train 8d (3p).

Whilst on the subject of football, on 16th February 1935, Keynsham played at home against Clevedon in the fourth round of the Somerset Senior Cup. There were cheap day return tickets from Clevedon to Keynsham on the 1.15pm and 2.2pm from Clevedon, arriving at Keynsham and Somerdale at 2.38 or 2.56pm respectively. A change of trains was necessary at Yatton, and again at Temple Meads on the 2.2pm departure. Return by any train the same day was permitted for a return fare of 2/- (10p). Keynsham won.

The semi-final, Keynsham v Frome was a three match event. The first match, at Frome, ended with a 2-2 draw. For the replay on Saturday, 23rd March, Keynsham and Somerdale was the destination for its very own excursion - possibly a unique event. The special train started at Frome at 1.50pm, calling at Bath at 2.35pm (fare 2/- 10p) arriving at Keynsham at 2.52pm, when the fare was half a crown (12$\frac{1}{2}$p) The return special was timed for 5.20pm, but in the event of extra time, departure would be delayed for 35 minutes. Amazingly, there was extra time when the 2-2 draw was converted during the extra time into a 3-3 draw, Frome equalising in the final two minutes of the game.

The second replay was at Radstock on the following Thursday, 28th March, when Keynsham won 3-2 after a 1-1 draw at half time. Although there was a one shilling (5p) advertised return fare from Frome, there is no record of any similar facility from Keynsham. Thursday was a working day, and in a time of high unemployment it would have been a brave man to have taken time off to watch football.

So, Keynsham made it to the final for the Somerset Senior Cup, it being reported that it was the first time Keynsham had ever got that far. Sadly, they lost 1-0 to Paulton

The excursion handbills for both the Keynsham and Paulton supporters' trains read as follows:

> Somerset Senior Cup Final at Wells
> Keynsham v Paulton Rovers
> Easter Monday April 22nd
> Half Day Excursion to Wells

Unfortunately, the railway got it wrong: the match was played two days earlier on Saturday, 20th April!

The return fare from Keynsham was 3/- (15p) Passengers changed trains at Temple Meads in each direction.

During the 1930s the Bristol Division published a series of three booklets setting out the Excursion Programmes, usually one for the summer service and others to cover the autumn and spring periods. The areas covered by the booklets were:

1. Bristol stations i.e. Parson Street to Severn Beach via both Clifton Down and Horfield, plus St Anne's Park.
2. Main line stations, Oldfield Park, Bath and stations to Swindon.
3. Everywhere else, which included Highbridge, Weston-super-Mare, the Weymouth line through Trowbridge, Frome, Yeovil, Maiden Newton and Dorchester. Also Keynsham and Saltford.

In consequence, Keynsham and Saltford often lost out. Many through excursion trains from Bristol called at St Anne's Park, then non-stop to Oldfield Park and Bath. In fact, that was nothing new, for back in January 1905 the Keynsham Parish Council wrote to the Great Western Railway asking for a better service than hitherto provided. It pointed out that Keynsham people often had to go to St Anne's Park (three miles) to get a train and then be brought back late at night. For most people that meant a three mile hike each way.

A classic example of the foregoing were the arrangements for the Silver Jubilee procession for King George V and Queen Mary on 6th June 1935. The excursion train left Weston super Mare at 5.50am, Temple Meads at 6.30am, Oldfield Park at 6.52am and Bath at 6.59am. Arrival at Paddington was at 9.2am. By that time, the processional route was packed to capacity and closed by the police to late arrivals. There were no bookings from Keynsham, although there were from such insignificant stations as Dauntsey (arrive Paddington 10.37) and Hallatrow (arrive Paddington 10.50)

For the Coronation on 12th May 1937 there was some improvement, but only some. The excursion left Temple Meads at midnight, called at Oldfield Park and Bath, arriving at Paddington at 3am. The return fare was 12/- (60p) from Temple Meads or 11/6 (57½p) Bath, and the return train 10.25pm. Keynsham folk had to pay 15/- (75p) for the privilege of travelling on ordinary service trains at 7.27am (Paddington 10am) or 9.1am (Paddington 12.30.) The return service was at 6.35pm, changing at Bath outward and Swindon return. However, all was not gloom. On Saturday 19th June 1937 there was the Coronation Tattoo at the Rushmoor Arena, Aldershot. The excursion train picked up at Keynsham at 2.45pm with an arrival at Aldershot (North Camp) at 5.50pm. The return train did not leave Aldershot until 1.35am and set down at Keynsham at 4.40am. Would folk do that to-day and then walk home from the station through unlit streets? Not really. If they were awake, those excursionists would have seen the dawn somewhere about Swindon and being June they would have walked home in broad daylight.

POST WAR

After the Second World War it took a few years for the railway to really get back into the excursion business. Time was needed to recover from the run down state of track, locomotives and rolling stock. For six long years only essential maintenance had been carried out and most bomb damage repair work needed upgrading to acceptable peace time standards. To illustrate the cautious return to normal conditions, there were commencing on 1st August 1946, day excursion tickets on Tuesdays, Wednesdays and Thursdays only to Weston-super-Mare. Travel was only permitted outward on the 8.14am or 10.40am from Keynsham, returning home on the 5.10pm or 7.15pm from Weston. The fare was 4/3 (21p) return, 3rd-class only. The facilities were originally advertised until 3rd October, but later extended to 31st October.

Also from 1st August 1946, day excursion tickets were introduced on Tuesdays, Wednesdays and Thursdays only from Keynsham to Bath for 1/3 (6p) return and to Bristol at 9d (4p) return. The facilities were extended indefinitely from 8th October together with first class fares at 2/1 (10p) and 1/3 (6p) return respectively.

By the date of the Coronation, 2nd June 1953, things were just about back to normal. It was just about back to normal for Keynsham too! The special train to London (39/- [£1.95] first class, 26/- [£1.30] second class) left Temple Meads at 12.10am; calling at Oldfield Park and Bath, but not Keynsham. This time, at least, the participants got to London in time to secure a good position on the line of route for the procession. Two days later, a "Special Limited Evening Excursion" picked up at Keynsham at 3.50pm, arriving at Paddington at 6.25pm. The return train left Paddington at 12.20am, setting down at Keynsham at 3.10am. That would have given plenty of time to see the decorations, the illuminations, and the obligatory visit to the railings at Buckingham Palace. All for 52½p in today's money.

In the mid 1950s the railways latched on to organised day trips, providing trains on five consecutive days (Mondays to Fridays) from important centres of population to popular seaside resorts. Such trains were run during Wakes Weeks in the North and during the peak Bank Holiday week elsewhere. For example, one such train ran during 1957 as the "Somerset and Wilts Holiday Express",

complete with a large headboard on the front of the locomotive to that effect. It called at Keynsham. The five destinations were Porthcawl, Minehead, Weymouth, Exmouth and Bournemouth West — in that order. "Over 900 miles for 50/- (£2.50) said the blurb. Just 50p for each day's travel. Porthcawl has now vanished from the railway map, Bournemouth West is no more, and Minehead is at the end of the truncated West Somerset Railway from Bishop's Lydeard. Both, Weymouth and Exmouth stations have been moved slightly inland from their former sites and the land sold off for re-development. The trains ran for a number of years, but not always to the same destinations. There was about five hours at the seaside each day and everybody was home by 10pm. By booking in advance there were reserved seats, and should participants so desire, they could book for one or more individual days, but at a higher fare.

In 1957, in conjunction with P & A Campbell Ltd, there were combined tours from stations in the Bath and Bristol areas including Keynsham, to Barry (13/6 – 67p), Lynmouth (19/6 – 97p), Ilfracombe (19/6 – 97p) and Mumbles (19/6 – 97p) Passengers travelled to Weston-super-Mare by ordinary service trains and then had to find their own way to Birnbeck Pier. The recommended time to get to the pier was 45 minutes. There was a most intriguing footnote to the handbill; "Should the return boat not reach port in time to connect with the last train to destination, passengers will be allowed to proceed by the first available train the following day." The first train from Weston-super -Mare to Bristol was at 6am, so it would be interesting to learn where those who were unfortunate spent the night! On some dates the boat was not scheduled to dock at Birnbeck pier until between 9pm and 9.30pm. The last train for Keynsham and Bath left at 9.48pm and the last to Bristol at 10.40pm.

In 1965, there were "Go as you please Sunday Family Travel any Ten Sundays", 20th June to 5th September. That only allowed for two wet Sundays. Destinations available were Barry Island, Teignmouth, Dawlish, Exeter, Torquay, Paignton, Goodrington, Kingswear, Swindon and Weymouth. What would you do in Swindon on a wet Sunday in 1965? The fares were: 10

Sundays for £5 (once again 50p a day), 8 out of 10 for 85/- (£4.25), 6 out of 8 out for 70/- (£3.50) an 4 out of 6 for 50/- (£2.25). There were special reductions for families:

Dad/Mum/two children   One child free
Dad/Mum/four children   Two children free.

By the 1970s Keynsham had grown to become a sizeable and relatively affluent society. Therefore, the station was included in a wide range of excursion offers, notwithstanding that by that time the station was unstaffed and facilities minimal. Excursion trains between Bristol and Bath called to both pick up and set down, although on some occasions it was necessary to change trains at Temple Meads. Brochures were produced three times a year (early, summer and autumn), listing all special excursion trains which were being run in the Bristol area, with an alphabetical key to indicate which trains stopped where. For example, in the brochure covering the period January to June 1973, all trains which included the letter 'B' called at Keynsham and there were no fewer than 27 such trains. British Rail also latched on to current marketing techniques and promoted their wares under such titles as City Line, Coast Line, Holiday Preview and Merrymaker. City Line trains were destined for London, Birmingham or other large cities. Coast Line excursions went to such places as Eastbourne. Holiday Preview outings ran to popular holiday resorts during the early months of the year. Newquay on a wet Saturday afternoon could well persuade prospective holiday-makers to go to the Algarve instead! A reserved seat was provided on each train. Although less than twenty-five years ago, the fares look laughable, such have been the ravages of inflation. For example:

London	£1.40	Child £0.90
Weymouth	£0.95	£0.48
Oxford	£0.60	£0.40
Eastbourne	£1.60	£1.00
Grand National	£2.00	£1.50
Mystery	£1.40	£0.90

More exotic, on 14th April 1973 there was an excursion to West Cornwall and the Isles of Scilly, leaving Keynsham at 00.05 on the Saturday morning, back at 03.55 Sunday, by road from Temple Meads. The fare to West Cornwall at £3.50 included a coach tour to Lands End, St Ives and Falmouth extending from 10.00 until 18.00. The fare to the Scillies was £5, but you were on your own when you got there.

Provided the meals were booked in advance, there was breakfast on the forward Journey and supper on the return. The menus were:

Breakfast
    Cereal or Fruit Juice
    Grilled bacon, tomato, sausage, fried egg
    Toast, rolls, preserves
    Tea or coffee
Supper
    Oxtail soup, roll and butter
    Gammon steak, pineapple, tomato, fried egg, creamed potatoes
    Cheddar cheese and biscuits with celery

The charge per meal, including service charge was £1.10p per person. The probability was that it was served on proper china crockery instead of to-day's cardboard.

There was also a service of light refreshments in both directions.

1977 was the year of the Queen's Silver Jubilee. At last, Keynsham was recognised. The special train which left Temple Meads around 5am actually called to pick up. Arrival at Paddington at 7am gave ample time to obtain a reasonable viewpoint for the royal procession, for the crowds were not so thick as for the Jubilee of 1935 and the Coronations of 1937 and 1953. There were no restrictions on the trains for the return journey the same day. Day return tickets to Paddington were also available for use on any train except the 3.50am from Temple Meads.

During the early 1980s catchphrases were included on publicity material. There was Jimmy Savill with his "Have a Good Trip" (Hope it was not drugs) and followed later by "This is the Age of the Train" which, of course, could have more than one meaning. From 1979 until 1986, the Bitton Railway Company Limited (formerly the Bristol Suburban Railway Society) ran a series of imaginative excursions to attractive destinations. They were able to fill their trains, for a very modest fare, for which the excursionists were given at least three choices of destination. Being a railway society, the first choice was always a visit to a restored railway destination. The other choices were to spend time at one or more tourist centres, or a complete package which included a coach tour through delightful countryside (See Appendix B).

There were some interesting experiences on those excursions. On the very first the organisers had their baptism of trouble. On the outward journey the locomotive expired part way up the Lickey incline and needed to be pushed to the top. Thereafter it managed to cope with the mainly falling gradient to Saltley (Birmingham) where more time was lost whilst there was an exchange of locomotives. We arrived very late on to the North Yorkshire Moors Railway so that there was only ten minutes at our destination station at Grosmont, just enough time for the train to be reversed and our steam motive power to be attached to the front end, and for the return journey homewards. At York there was more trouble. At York a group of railwaymen and curious bystanders stood around a coach in the middle of our train whilst another railwayman wielded a large hammer underneath. The much banging and heaving proved fruitless and we eventually left York with one coach less than when we arrived. Home was two hours later than expected.

On 1st May 1982 the "Bitton Pennine" afforded the following choices:
(a) Alight at Keighley and spend the afternoon on the Worth Valley Railway (£9.45)
(b) Alight at Keighley for a round trip on the Worth Valley Railway, followed by a bus ride to Embsay for a round trip on the Yorkshire Dales Railway (£11.45)
(c) Spend the afternoon at Skipton (£8.25) or Carlisle (£8.95) or
(d) Alight at Garsdale for a coach trip through the Yorkshire Dales and back to Skipton via Kettlewell and Bolton Abbey (£10.45).
We selected the coach tour and upon arrival at Garsdale we viewed with some wonder the elderly buses which were to convey us on our "coach tour". Our wonder was not misplaced when our particular "coach" expired on one of the very steep inclines which abounded on our very scenic route. Like the locomotive on the Lickey, our vehicle recovered sufficiently to complete the journey, but only after we had all alighted and walked to the top of the hill.

On the "Bitton Conwy Express", which ran on 1st June 1985, the choices were even better:
(a) Spend the afternoon at Chester (£9.50), Llandudno (£10.50) or Blaenau Ffestiniog (£11.00)
(b) A trip on the narrow gauge Ffestiniog Railway from Blaenau Ffestiniog to Porthmadog and back (£14.00)
(c) A visit to the Llechwedd Slate Caverns at Blaenau Ffestiniog (£14.00)
(d) A coach tour from Llandudno Junction to Snowdonia (£12.00)
(e) By coach from Llandudno Junction to Llanberis for a return trip on the Snowdon Mountain Railway (£15.00).

On that occasion we selected one of the first choices and alighted at Blaenau Ffestiniog. We joined the Porthmadog bound Ffestiniog Railway train and were the only passengers to alight at the first station stop at Tan-y-Grisiau. Tan-y-Grisiau is 640ft above sea level, and here we boarded a Crosville bus to take us a further 1,000ft up the mountain to the Stwlan Dam. Compared to the oppressive heat of the summer afternoon down below, we enjoyed, in almost splendid isolation, the balmy air and the panoramic vista which was such a contrast to the traffic-clogged and fume-laden atmosphere of Keynsham High Street. All for £11 each on a day out.

The Bitton people ran eighteen trains over the eight years. All except three trains started at Taunton and picked up passengers at stations between Castle Cary and Bristol Temple Meads via Trowbridge and Bath. The first two trains also started at Taunton but ran main line to Bristol with connections from the Bath direction. Three trains ran on Sundays, the remainder on Saturdays. Sadly, British Rail increased their charge to the point where the Bitton Company could no longer charge economic fares to their regular clientele.

It was at this period that the railways virtually withdrew from the traditional special excursion train programme in favour of the chartered train concept, i.e. let somebody else do all the organising and take the financial risks. That concept has left the business sectors with only a limited fleet of spare rolling stock, plus the problem of a shortage of train crews in many areas. The traditional railway excursion is, alas, no more.

Fairburn 2–6–4T 2085 in Caledonian blue livery at Lakeside station on the Lakeside and Haverthwaite Railway on the occasion of the Bitton Railway Co's visit on 10th May 1986.   *Author*

1977
excursion
handbill

1983
excursion
handbill

13. Commercial Performance

Annual statistical traffic returns for all individual stations in the Bristol Division are preserved at the Public Record Office at Kew. The statistics relating to Keynsham have been summarised and are reproduced at Appendix C. From 1907 until 1924 only figures relating to revenue are shown. From 1925 until 1949 pre-printed forms were used so that much more supporting detail is available, such as the number of passengers and the tonnage of merchandise dealt with. Subsequent to 1949 all goods traffic was zoned, so that figures for stations such as Keynsham are not available. Passenger returns are available until 1959.

Until the First World War the indications are of traffic not showing much variation between one year and another, despite the provision of a new goods yard in 1911. (Total revenue, goods and passenger was £10,164 in 1907 and £10,645 in 1914.) It was not until after the cessation of hostilities that the railways were able to raise their passenger fares and goods rates to allow for the impact of inflation. The result was that gross revenue almost doubled from £15,763 in 1918 to £29,942 in 1920. The immediate succeeding years were years of deflation when fares and rates gradually returned towards pre-war levels. Co-incidental with that were the intermittent reductions in rates of pay which were tied into a reducing percentage increase in the cost of living over pre-war levels.

Passenger

The number of passengers recorded on the pre-printed forms excludes season ticket holders and represents the number of tickets sold rather than journeys made. That will account for the fact that the influx of Fry's employees during the 1920s had only a limited impact on the number of tickets sold: the vast majority of employees would have travelled to Keynsham with return tickets. On the other hand, there were available cheap single tickets for Fry's employees, for example, in the 1950s there was a six-penny single to Temple Meads, against the normal single fare of nine pence.

Interpretation of passenger statistics post 1924 is not straightforward, being affected by the gradual increase in the Keynsham population on the one hand and the transfer to cars and buses on the other. Inevitably, war time conditions and the ravages of inflation also had a significant impact. There is also the possibility of statistical error, so that passenger numbers recorded for 1925, 1926 and 1927 at 102,046, 88,863 and 100,035 respectively make 1926 look suspicious, until it is remembered that 1926 was the year of the general strike. After 1927 the passenger figures fluctuated, generally not far below 90,000 until 1935 at 89,055. The following three years indicates a general fall off, counterbalanced by an increase in season tickets.

The massive increase in passenger numbers from 87,623 in 1940 to 125,798 in 1941 coincided with the blitz on Bristol and Bath in the temporary overnight evacuation into the surrounding countryside. There were no day return tickets; (suspended for the duration of the war) evacuees purchased either single or full fare returns into Bristol or Bath each morning. The suspension of day return tickets accounts for the corresponding increase in income, clearly shown by comparing the years 1940 £3,922 for 87,623 tickets and in 1942, £5,873 for 88,504 tickets. Put another way, the average price for each ticket sold was (in to-day's money) 38p in 1925, 40p in 1938, 66p in 1942 and £1.15 in 1945.

Turning now to season tickets, these tended to gradually increase over the years, from 2,521 in 1927 to 2,831 in 1938. The average price of a season ticket in 1927 was 57p (in to-day's money) and down to 36p in 1938, a mixture of annual, quarterly, monthly or weekly tickets. The lesser averages over the years are probably accounted for by the loss of first class patrons, the more affluent who transferred to their private cars. The figures may look ridiculous, but in 1949 the cost of a weekly season from Keynsham to Bath was only 7/9 (39p) compared with £13 in 1996! Petrol rationing brought the car owners back to the railway so that the number of season tickets issued soared from the 2,831 in 1938 to 3,546 in the following year and to a peak of 4,432 in 1943. From that peak, there was a reduction in number every year for the next eleven years, so that by 1954 only 640 season tickets were sold. For the last year for which statistics are available, 1959, the total was down to 496. On the other hand, ticket sales, although fluctuating from year to year, held up quite well. In 1959 60,664 tickets were sold, attracting an income of £5,466, an average of 90p per ticket, a significant reduction from war time prices, indicating the principal sales were day returns and the restoration of cheap excursion fares after the war.

Parcels
The arrival of Fry's in the 1920s and the Keynsham Paper Mill in 1933 both had their influence upon volume, but only significantly on incoming traffic. There was a temporary increase in parcels forwarded during 1931 and 1932. On 13th September 1932, Messrs J.S. Fry & Sons inaugurated an air service from Somerdale for urgent requirements. An aeroplane loaned from the Bristol Airport at Whitchurch, was utilised for the initial flight and Lord Apsley officiated on behalf of the Air Ministry. The innovation was stated to be an experiment and only infrequent trips were made.[1] It is doubtful if the experiment had any significant impact upon the railway's statistics, but it does indicate that Fry's were looking for some alternative mode for the despatch of parcels.

The revenue received from parcels traffic was significantly reduced after 1934 because all incoming traffic then became prepaid.

Coal
The gradual build up of chocolate production at Fry's is clearly reflected in the increase in coal tonnage up to and including 1932. The following year marked the start of production at the Keynsham Paper Mill.

General Merchandise
As with coal, the influence of Fry's and the Keynsham Paper Mill is very marked, that being particularly so with the "not carted" category, i.e. the tonnage accounted for at

Keynsham, but shunted directly into their private sidings. The tonnage figures for 1940 are extraordinary with the tonnage carted almost quadrupled, but reverting to normal in 1941. It could have been in connection with war time armaments, or very possibly a serious statistical error attributed to inexperienced war time clerical staff.

In the quarter century 1925-49 some 1,874,551 tons of merchandise passed through the books at Keynsham Goods, of which almost half a million tons was coal.

Lavatories
The few pounds sterling of income from lavatories cannot go without comment, despite its insignificance compared with the tens of thousand pounds generated from other sources. Somebody, somewhere, seems to have had an obsession with the subject and it is faithfully recorded, station by station, in the Divisional Manager's Annual Report to Paddington, and, from 1925 forward, on the official pre-printed returns. The Divisional Manager's Annual Report even went as far as to record the daily takings during Bank Holiday periods at the Locking Road excursion platforms at Weston-super-Mare. For example, on August Bank Holiday Monday 1933, no fewer than 1,345 people spent a penny (£5.12s 1d) [£5.60] and the comparative figure for 1932 was given as 1,409 people, generating an income of £5.17s 5d [£5.87]. No doubt, the actual figure for usage was much higher, taking into account those who nipped in before the door closed on the previous departing occupant!

The annual figures returned for Keynsham show high usage during the war years, no doubt because facilities at home were not available. The reason for a higher income during the 1950s is less obvious for the establishments were far from palatial.

PRO references:
    1907-24   Rail 253/529 to 544
    1925-59   Rail 266/57 and 72 to 74

---

[1]PRO Rail 253/552.

14. The Proposed Closure of the Station

The crunch came in October 1968 when notices appeared proposing to discontinue passenger services from a whole string of stations between Bristol and Weymouth, including Keynsham. As far as the northern end of the line was concerned, the TUCC hearing was only three months later, on 21st January 1969, held in the Concert Room of the Pump Room in Bath. Indeed, it was only a "hearing". The Committee listened to a succession of objectors, ranging from the Clerk to the Keynsham Urban District Council, down to a commuting schoolgirl. The one important missing objector was J.S. Fry & Sons who were quite prepared to take the bus company's word that they would be able to provide the necessary alternative transport. In fact, the bus company's representative had the audacity to say that they could cope with the additional traffic arising from the proposed station closures, when every objector present knew full well that they could not cope with the traffic they already had. Cancellation of peak hour bus journeys was endemic due to staff shortages, for this was a period of full employment and, especially in summer, coach driving was more lucrative than bus driving. The other big problem was traffic congestion when, during the morning and evening peaks, it could take up to 45 minutes to cover the five miles between Bristol and Keynsham, a situation which can still arise to-day. The traffic problems of the day were compounded as a result of the flood disaster the previous July when all the town bridges in Keynsham were washed away, the temporary replacements being Bailey bridges provided by the Army.

The "hearing" conveniently ended about 12.45, the objectors went their several ways and, presumably, the Committee went off to lunch. As was normal on those occasions,

---

NATIONAL UNION OF RAILWAYMEN
BRISTOL DISTRICT COUNCIL

WITHDRAWAL OF RAILWAY PASSENGER SERVICE

St. Annes Park, Keynsham/Somerdale, Saltford and Oldfield Park

Any user or body representing such users may lodge objections to any of these station closures.

You may do so if any HARDSHIP, such as personal inconvenience, longer time in travel, cost, employment, schoolchildren, recreation, etc. are involved.

This is your democratic right, USE IT and retain your RAILWAY SERVICE, ITS UP TO YOU.

Lodge your objection in WRITING NOT LATER than 30th NOVEMBER 1968.

Addressed to:
The Secretary,
Transport Users Consultative Committee for
the South Western Area,
Magnet House,
32 Victoria Street,
BRISTOL 1.

Remember

If no objections are lodged to the proposal the STATIONS will be CLOSED on 6th JANUARY 1969.

Don't leave it to someone else --
You do it NOW

The downside platform level view of Keynsham station in the year of proposed closure – 1969. *Author*

objectors could not be challenged, there was no cross examination, objectors just said their piece and that was that. It was, indeed, just a "hearing".

Following the "hearing" there was a long period of silence, as was normal in the circumstances. In the following October there was a report in the local newspaper stating that Keynsham station, together with 14 others, would be unstaffed from the following Monday. That upset the Urban District Council, for that was the first they had heard of the proposal. There was also a widespread feeling that such action foretold of the imminent closure of the stations concerned. That, of course, was denied, although for some of the stations concerned, it turned out to be true.

When the stock of day-return tickets from Keynsham to Bath ran out some weeks prior to destaffing, it then became obvious that the decision to destaff had been taken several months earlier. Recourse was made to the issue of single tickets overstamped "Return". When they ran out paper Excess Fare tickets were used. When they ran out, for a couple of days until new pads of paper tickets could be obtained, it was "'Pay at the other end".

From the Heads of Information prepared by the railway, and supplied to objectors prior to the Hearing, the daily average station use by fare paying passengers for the week commencing 10th June 1968, was 108 joining and 117 leaving trains at Keynsham. Total 225. As most of the passengers probably made return journeys, the number of people using the trains was somewhere around 120. Of those 225 joining or leaving, 45 arrived at 07.19 (06.33 from Avonmouth) and 22 on the 07.24 arrival (06.20 from Frome). 44 joined the 17.14 to Avonmouth and a further 15 the 17.27 to Bath and Weymouth. Thus, more than half the patronage came from four trains and they were almost wholly Fry's workers. That left for the remaining 17 trains that called, 49 passengers joining and 50 leaving, the average per train being 2.8 and 2.9 respectively.

In addition there were 109 railwaymen who held residential free passes, some of whom were regular users of the trains. Regular or not, they had no say in the matter. The figures were pretty depressing, the case looked hopeless, we feared the worst. We did not have long to wait for the first shock came within a week of the hearing, when the Western Region published their new timetable, operative from 5th May 1969. The train service to local stations between Bristol and Bath had been slashed. The best patronised train of the day at 17.18 from Bristol was taken off, leaving passengers with a choice at 16.55 or 17.50, neither of which would be acceptable to the majority. From Bath, there was to be no train calling at Keynsham between departures at 17.00 and 18.42.

The railway had already been accused of being dishonest in the presentation of its case at the TUCC Hearing. It now became apparent that there had been a deliberate suppression of information so that the timetable detail presented, without a hint of things to come, was, to say the least, misleading.

The voices of protest were soon raised and the author, for one, had correspondence with the railway, the TUCC and with Mr (now Sir) Paul Dean, the local Member of Parliament. The substance of the railway's response was unsatisfactory, the TUCC were non committal, as no doubt they had to be, passing my letters on to the Minister. Paul Dean was most helpful. Three months later, and only a week prior to the introduction of the new timetable, a pamphlet appeared advertising three additional peak hour trains each way between Bristol and Bath. Included was the reinstated 17.18 from Bristol and a 17.20 from Bath. We had won: but it proved to be only the first round.

The Minister of Transport, Mr Fred Mulley, eventually gave his verdict on 5th November 1969. The relevant paragraph concerning Keynsham said:

"He had noted the Committee's view that there would be hardship for a relatively small number of people in the event of closure. The Minister considers that the existing frequent alternative bus services would in the normal course of events provide an adequate alternative means of public transport. However, bearing in mind the current problems of road congestion, which may be made more acute by major road works now in progress, he feels that it would be right at the present time to maintain a peak hour rail service for the majority of regular rail users. In this connection he understands it would be possible to withdraw the local train service between Bristol and Bath, whilst still providing rail services for the bulk of peak hour travellers by stopping certain main line trains at suitable times at the two most used stations, namely Keynsham and Somerdale and Oldfield Park. I am to invite the Board to publish details of the proposed service as soon as possible".

A legacy of the July 1968 flood disaster was the necessity to reconstruct the town centre main road bridge over the River Chew, that being the major road work to which reference was made. It was that which saved the day for Keynsham station.

Having received the verdict, a spiteful British Rail once again got their Dirty Tricks Department to devise a timetable that suited the least possible number of passengers. It is reproduced overleaf, from which it will be seen that there would be no arrival in Bristol between 07.59 and 09.00 and no departure in the evening after 16.55. Bath was no better, with no departure between 17.00 and 18.35. In short, the timetable was useless for office and shop workers commuting to Bristol or Bath. However, it did provide a service for Fry's workers coming out from Bristol and Bath, but nothing to cater for the early finish on Fridays. The timetable was dated to commence on 5th January 1970.

		Mondays to Fridays					Saturdays	
Bath Spa	dpt	07.12	07.34	08.35	17.00	18.35	08.35	13.25
Oldfield Park	dpt	07.15	07.37	08.38	17.03	18.38	08.38	13.28
Keynsham & Somerdale	dpt	07.25	07.47	08.48	17.14	18.48	08.48	13.39
Bristol Temple Meads	arr	07.37	07.59	09.00	17.28	19.00	08.58	13.50
Bristol Temple Meads	dpt	06.20	07.05	07.50	15.40	16.55	12.34	16.55
Keynsham & Somerdale	dpt	06.29	07.15	08.01	15.51	17.05	12.45	17.05
Oldfield Park	dpt	–	–	08.12	16.02	17.15	12.56	17.15
Bath Spa	arr	06.39	–	08.15	16.05	17.19	12.59	17.19

Needless to say, voices of protest were raised again, joined this time by that of the Urban District Council. Once more, the local MP was most helpful. The outcome was that stops were reinstated into the 07.30 from Frome at Oldfield Park and at 08.14 at Keynsham for Bristol bound passengers. There was also an additional train provided for homeward bound passengers at 17.40 from Temple Meads.

TAILPIECE
When the Urban District Council was discussing, and objecting to the proposed closure, Cllr Douglas Miles asked if the two local stations (Keynsham and Saltford) could be preserved until the day came when commuters were fed up with congested roads and wanted to return to rail travel. Truly prophetic.

The half demolished up side station building on 11th June 1970, less than twelve months after the date of the official reprieval of the passenger service.

15. After 1969

Having lost the day concerning closure, the railway lost no time in reducing what was left of the station "amenities". By May 1970 the station footbridge had been dismantled and sold to the Dart Valley Railway. It has been re-erected at their Buckfastleigh station. The derelict station buildings were demolished, although their awnings did give some protection from the elements. Some of the ugly corrugated awning (with accompanying colander effect) which was erected when the station was enlarged in the early thirties was left in situ, but badly situated at the far Bristol end of the long platforms. Both platforms were left completely bare and there were no seats. The only decorative feature was that liberally provided by the local graffiti artists.

To that uninviting station came Her Majesty the Queen during one of her Silver Jubilee tours in 1977. She arrived by road from Bath on Tuesday afternoon, 8th August to join the royal train which, that day, had been made up by BR with prestige vehicles from their new toy. There were four HST first class trailers, a catering vehicle and power cars 253 025, one at each end. Her Majesty was heard to remark that it was not her usual train and probably the significance of the power car numbers was lost upon most observers.

Her Majesty, having negotiated two flights of bare concrete steps to reach the platform, found a bit of red carpet which did little to improve the drab surroundings. However, like Alice in Wonderland, the painters had been there the previous Sunday, not to paint white roses red (of course there were no roses to paint) but to paint out the graffiti. No doubt, Her Majesty had no wish to be informed that "Bristol Ruals."

At the foot of the steps, and to hopefully deflect her gaze from the surrounding drabness, there was a departure from tradition. Instead of a bouquet of flowers, Her Majesty was presented with a box of Fry's chocolates for her to enjoy en route to her next engagement at Weston-super-Mare. Whether she did, or not, is not recorded, but it has been established that prior to that evening's Reception on the Royal Yacht, Prince Edward

(then a lad of 13) had already enjoyed his share of the contents.

Once the problems with the abortive closure proposals were sorted out, the timetable settled down to a truly abysmal level for the next twelve years. The timetable reproduced overleaf is representative of the whole period, the times of the trains (with one exception) varying only by a few minutes year by year in the normal manner associated with railway timetables, and to the chagrin of regular last-minuters when the departure time has been advanced by, say, two minutes.

H.M. The Queen receiving a box of Fry's chocolates from Mrs Dorothy Rudderham, Chairperson Wansdyke District Council on the bare down platform of Keynsham station. 8th August 1977.
Bristol Evening Post

115

May 1974 until May 1975

Up Trains	From	Time at Keynsham	To	
	Bristol	06.57	Portsmouth Harbour	
	Severn Beach	*07.21 SX*	*Keynsham*	*via Temple Meads*
	Bristol	07.22 SO	Portsmouth Harbour (until 28th Sept)	
	Bristol	08.15	Weymouth (SX until 28th Sept)	
	Bristol	13.07 SO	Portsmouth Harbour	
	Bristol	16.08	Weymouth	(Portsmouth Harbour SO until 28th September)
	Bristol	*17.12*	*Portsmouth Harbour*	
	Bristol	17.52	Weymouth	

Down Trains				
	Westbury	*07.15*	*Bristol*	
	Swindon	07.41 SX	Bristol	
	Weymouth	08.32	Bristol	
	Portsmouth Harbour	14.08 SO	Bristol	
	Westbury	*17.16*	*Severn Beach*	(SX until 28th Sept)
	Weymouth	18.42	Bristol	(SX until 28th Sept)

No Sunday Service
Fry's Worker Trains shown in italics

In summary, there was no train to Bristol after 14.08 on Saturdays, later amended to 14.51. On normal week-days there was no train to Bristol after 08.32 until 17.16 and none to Bath between 08.15 and 17.12.

In the early 1980s there was an explosion of interest in city centre transport problems by provincial urban local authorities. On the other hand, motorists began to experience the worsening uncertainties of journey times due to traffic congestion and an escalation of city centre parking charges. The uncertainties experienced by motorists were felt equally by those who commuted by bus which also had a knock on effect upon timekeeping and timetables. Nobody in authority seems to have done anything to turn the tide from road to rail in those early days; it was just as imperceptible as the ocean tide; then it just gathered momentum as indeed the tide does at Weston-super-Mare.

Business at Keynsham just started to grow, so that in May 1982 an additional stop was introduced into an existing non-stop service at 08.20 in order to relieve the pressure on the following 08.30. In October 1983 that train was taken off and Keynsham passengers had the luxury of HST travel on the 06.35 from Paddington. That train was, in turn, taken off in May 1987 for lack of patronage at the London end and the service reverted to locomotive and coaches Swindon to Taunton.

Avon County Council were early on the scene promoting improvements to local stations in partnership with British Rail and in accordance with the County's Official Structure Plan. Keynsham's turn came in December 1983, with the Press announcement that Avon were to contribute £110,000 for improvement to stations between Bristol and Freshford. (Freshford was the last station geographically within the former Avon County).

The first visible evidence of Avon County's promised interest in Keynsham station was the arrival, in pieces, of a surplus pedestrian bridge that once spanned Penn Street in central Bristol. Delivery was made on Sunday 29th January 1984. Notice was given that the car park (such as it was) would be closed that day because of the presence of a crane.

The only action during the ensuing twelve months was the felling of the tall trees at the

 *Author*

rear of the up side platform to provide room for the bridge approach steps. The bridge was erected during April/May 1985. Unfortunately, when erected, a 7" gap became evident between the top of the steps and the crossing section above the line. Poor chap, it was said that the erection of the bridge was a young engineer's first project.

Following on from the footbridge, the station car park was taken in hand during the period October to December 1985. Up to that date, there had been a bit of rough land which provided parking space for about 20 vehicles. That area was fenced off during the period of construction.

Fry's former siding was filled in and the whole was levelled off and properly surfaced, including the space once occupied by the loading dock siding which had been filled with rubble from the 1971 demolition. The capacity of the parking area was trebled, but was full by 08.30 on most Monday to Friday mornings. That was until the opening of the Avon County Park and Ride facility at Brislington in late 1993 and the opening of the Avon Ring Road in early 1994. (see also Chapter 19). Until then a significant number of people drove over to Keynsham from Longwell Green, Oldland and Willsbridge, locations on the Gloucestershire side of the river, where there has been widespread housing development in recent years.

In addition to the car park, and as part of the same project, a waiting shelter was constructed adjacent to the up side platform entrance and to the new footbridge. To complete that part of the station refurbishment the platform area was resurfaced. Finally, during 1988, the waste land beside the footbridge steps was landscaped by the planting of suitable bushes. The up side of the station now has a very presentable appearance; the down side is just as the demolition contractors left it twenty-five years ago.

With the upsurge of morning commuter traffic, it was in 1983 that a man was sent out from Bristol to issue tickets, arriving by train at 7.12 and returning to Bristol on the 8.30,

117

Keynsham station in January 1986 showing the new up side passenger shelter, the bottom steps of the new footbridge, the 113¾ milepost and the well filled car park.   *Author*

subsequently extended to 10.04. In June 1984 a portable ticket office was delivered for the use of, and greater comfort of, the said man. Initially it was positioned at the bottom of the steps on the down side — until it was overturned by vandals. It has since been repositioned at the top of the steps on the down side, a position much more convenient for passengers travelling in the direction of Bath. There is now installed within, a telephone and a portable electric heater.

By the summer of 1985 there were seventeen trains each day calling at Keynsham. Then handbills were produced with a great flourish to announce that from 30th September of that year the number of trains calling would be increased to 24, one of which was the 05.18 to Westbury and another the 06.07 to Weymouth! However, better things were in store, so that by the summer of 1989 the number of trains calling had increased to 45 and to 47 in the winter timetable for 1994/95 — the best service

for over 30 years. Most of the trains in the Bath direction continue to Portsmouth Harbour or Weymouth, and in the opposite direction, many continue to Cardiff. Until 1992, there was even a through service at 07.26 to Manchester.

In October 1989, Mr Mervyn Cross was appointed as a part time booking clerk. He travels out from Bath on the first morning train and returns to Bath by train at 10.40. Mr Cross used to run a public house, and he brings to Keynsham station the true jovial nature of mine host. He is a credit to BR.

One time problems of overcrowding during the morning peak have been alleviated, but occasionally trains to Bristol are already full and standing when they arrive at Keynsham. Off peak patronage is thin, although there has built up a healthy trade in longer distance travel, particularly when through services are available. The percentage of the total Keynsham population who use the trains is

Avon Rail Stations Passenger Census

PASSENGERS BOARDING AND ALIGHTING AT ALL STATIONS IN AVON (a)

COUNTY OF AVON
BRITISH RAIL WESTERN REGION

Autumn 1987
Survey Date – Tuesday 10 November 1987
Weather – Intermittant rain am, sunny pm

No. of trains surveyed Nov 1987	Station		1987 Nov	1987 Aug	1986 Nov	1986 Aug	1985 Nov	1985 Aug	1984 Nov	1984 Aug	1983 Nov	1983 Aug	1982 Nov	1982 Aug	1981 Nov	1981 Aug	1980 Nov	1980 Aug	1979 Nov	1979 Aug
81 (b)	Bristol Parkway		4801	4387	4591	4598	3928	4086	3765	3535	3231	3515	3141	2868	2316	2524	2903	2625	2666	1970
7	Pilning		3	2	0	2	2	1	2	3	2	3	5	7	2	9	4	13	3	9
8	Patchway		16	13	23	14	26	20	21	17	25	20	19	16	35	29	24	45	41	26
9	Filton		24	31	23	17	28	31	29	16	32	37	22	20	39	30	27	27	44	36
36	Severn Beach		190	278	168	262	173	220	180	255	161	224	165	178	216	245	189	269	200	206
36	St Andrews Road		71	58	61	60	92	71	59	64	68	84	87	62	69	78	79	93	68	69
36	Avonmouth		22	231	248	248	257	246	237	280	277	270	298	220	337	282	327	321	357	297
	Shirehampton		202	185	189	197	195	240	216	214	171	196	202	196	223	212	214	195	177	136
36	Sea Mills		167	136	157	134	155	162	178	130	220	144	207	122	172	131	167	111	165	68
36	Clifton Down		506	441	479	361	460	399	416	405	446	367	430	278	417	315	306	284	262	252
36	Redland		187	232	189	189	224	179	195	173	187	122	155	99	146	165	158	141	168	126
36	Montpelier		232	176	274	152	251	166	225	133	247	138	194	140	179	142	160	163	163	84
11	Stapleton Road	N	23	24	24	33	42	32	32	39	43	43	21	24	31	61	69	89	51	72
36	Stapleton Road	S	280	249	247	202	214	216	209	187	206	154	215	173	231	181	171	208	148	173
6	Lawrence Hill	N	7	7	12	7	20	23	25	23	23	31	40	23	57	40	66	51	24	53
36	Lawrence Hill	S	200	211	173	256	210	187	166	205	181	172	167	122	140	213	148	200	158	176
36 (a)	Bristol Temple Meads	S	480	570	509	537	499	543	511	540	510	485	508	482	506	725	456	573	405	441
10	Bedminster		49	49	43	48	49	58	30	25	28	17	35	26	38	38	79	39	61	60
9	Parson Street		31	31	38	23	50	61	36	92	46	77	37	45	35	135	46	60	35	59
43 (d)	Nailsea & Blackwell		766	685	640	593	693	579	659	508	674	576	521	476	508	488	480	399	493	426
43 (d)	Yatton		861	839	821	733	870	643	723	709	709	730	702	668	681	807	828	734	811	815
43 (d)	Weston Milton		440	319	394	385	453	323	439	367	402	362	403	290	421	327	455	336	440	338
49 (d)	Weston-super-Mare		1409	3272	1369	3113	1416	3843	1350	3070	1426	3826	1624	3868	1385	5258	1986	4331	1811	4118
32	Keynsham		594	396	561	424	450	303	356	303	323	333	299	252	360	249	345	291	306	22
17	Oldfield Park		281	210	202	171	213	183	164	180	158	179	138	121	162	165	169	176	163	139
83 (c)	Bath Spa		7819	8979	7893	8361	7428	7895	6155	7548	6348	7548	6394	6869	5339	7293	6545	6690	5636	6910
8	Freshford		46	36	35	19	38	31	32	18	39	25	36	21	26	25	28	N/SVD	18	18
	Severn Beach Line		2736	2767	2694	2598	2730	2629	2592	2386	2674	2356	2628	2072	2636	2662	2444	2366	2206	2058
	Other Stations		17170	19940	16869	18761	15730	18606	14918	16858	13357	17367	13472	15619	13626	17533	14054	15906	12684	15379
	Total less Pkway Bath		7286	8841	7079	8200	7104	8792	6520	7994	6645	8860	6565	7954	6507	10378	7050	9157	6588	8557
	GRAND TOTAL		19906	22207	19563	21359	18460	21235	17510	19444	16031	19723	16100	17691	14162	20195	16498	18472	14890	17437

NOTES

N = Cardiff/Parkway Services
S = Severn Beach Line Services

(a) At Bristol Temple Meads, only Severn Beach line services have been surveyed; all other train calls in Avon, except those noted below, were covered in Summer 1987.
(b) 0115 to Cardiff from London not covered.
(c) 0205 to Penzance from London, 0353 to London from Penzance, 0357 to Bristol from Southampton not covered.
(d) 0736 Highbridge - Swindon did not run west of Bristol.

Courtesy British Rail

very small indeed, perhaps, less than 2%. For those who use public transport, the station is inconveniently situated on the northern edge of the town and at Bristol, Temple Meads, is a mile from the commercial and shopping centres. Furthermore, there are frequent bus services right on the doorstep and right into the centre of town. As we saw back in 1969 with the threat of closure, if British Rail should at any time cut back at Keynsham, it will not be those who use the trains who will necessarily make the most noise.

Before leaving consideration of the regular train services, it is appropriate to mention that apart from the summer Sunday Weymouth excursions, there had been no Sunday trains calling at Keynsham since 1964. Sunday trains were re-introduced with the October 1985 timetable, three trains in each direction. By the summer of 1989 the trains had increased to 17 and by the winter of 1994 to 18.

To support the glowing picture just narrated, British Rail have kindly supplied census counts for passengers using all stations in the County of Avon, covering the years 1979 to 1987. Excluding the main stations of Temple Meads, Parkway and Bath Spa, there are 22 stations listed and Keynsham ranked fourth in November 1987. It was a straight count, therefore the majority of passengers will have been counted twice, both outward and return. The figure of 306 in November 1979 had only increased to 356 five years later, then it was 1985 – 450; 1986 – 561; and 1987 – 594. Reverting to 1968, and excluding the defunct Fry's passenger traffic, the comparative figure was 119. Therefore, passenger traffic increased fivefold in twenty years.

An increase in local rail traffic was not peculiar to Keynsham. It is occurring up and down the land. Two reasons are suggested. First, the certainty of peak hour congestion and frustration on the road and the steep increases that have taken place in car parking charges in city centres; BR cashing in by the provision of free parking at suburban stations.

Winter service 1987/88

The timetable for the winter of 1987/88 was the last before the second generation dmus took over. It was dominated on week-days by the hourly Portsmouth line service with, generally speaking, alternate trains calling at Keynsham. Included therein were two trains in each direction to and from Brighton, but only one, the 11.40 to Cardiff called at Keynsham. In the other direction only, there were two trains which originated at Swansea. Weymouth was still very poorly served, for there was no suitable direct train from Keynsham for a day out at the seaside.

The most notable feature of the rostering arrangements was the predominance of locomotive hauled trains in the hands of Southern Region Cl. 33s. It was the general practice that a second member of the class took over when the train reversed direction at Temple Meads for the Cardiff leg of the journey. Such was the predominance of

Mervyn Cross (better known as Merv) in his portable ticket office on 28th February 1991. *Author*

Winter Service at Keynsham 1987-8

Up trains

Rostered for	From	Time at Keynsham	To
33	Bristol	05.08	Yeovil
dmu	Bristol Parkway	06.03	Weymouth
33	Cardiff	07.11	Portsmouth Harbour
33	Cardiff	08.04	Portsmouth Harbour
dmu	Weston-super-Mare	08.32	Swindon
dmu	Bristol	08.59	Swindon
33	Bristol	10.16	Portsmouth Harbour
33	Swansea	12.13	Portsmouth Harbour
33	Cardiff	14.13	Portsmouth Harbour
33	Bristol	16.23	Weymouth
dmu	Bristol	17.12 SX	Bath
33	Cardiff	17.26	Portsmouth Harbour
dmu	Bristol	17.53	Frome
33	Swansea	18.18	Portsmouth Harbour
33	Bristol	20.23	Portsmouth Harbour
dmu	Bristol	21.53 SX	Westbury
dmu	Bristol	22.03 SO	Westbury
dmu	Bristol	23.17	Swindon (SX from 6th Feb)
bus	Bristol	23.25 SO	Swindon (from 6th Feb)

Sundays

33	Cardiff	17.08	Portsmouth Harbour
33	Cardiff	20.18	Portsmouth Harbour
33	Cardiff	22.03	Portsmouth Harbour

Winter Service at Keynsham 1987-8

Down trains Rostered for	From	Time at Keynsham	To
dmu	Frome	07.04	Bristol Parkway
dmu	Swindon	07.24	Penzance
dmu	Swindon	08.07	Taunton
33	Yeovil	08.27	Bristol
33	Portsmouth Harbour	09.40	Cardiff
33	Brighton	11.40	Cardiff
33	Portsmouth Harbour	13.35	Cardiff
33	Portsmouth Harbour	15.35	Bristol
33	Portsmouth Harbour	16.30	Cardiff
33	Portsmouth Harbour	17.43	Bristol
33	Portsmouth Harbour	18.36	Cardiff
33	Portsmouth Harbour	19.42	Cardiff
33	Portsmouth Harbour	20.36	Cardiff
33	Weymouth	21.47	Bristol
33	Portsmouth Harbour	23.01 SX	Cardiff
33	Portsmouth Harbour	23.01 SO	Cardiff (until 26th Dec)
33	Portsmouth Harbour	23.01 SO	Bristol (2nd until 30th Jan)
bus	Westbury	23.35 SO	Bristol (from 6th Feb)

Sundays

33	Portsmouth Harbour	18.43	Cardiff
33	Weymouth	20.17	Bristol
33	Portsmouth Harbour	21.45	Cardiff

Cl. 33s that on occasions half a dozen could be seen at one time on Bristol Bath Road depot.

The few remaining trains that called at Keynsham were worked by what we now know as heritage dmus, and therein was included one early morning train through from Swindon to Penzance.

A feature we have not seen in the earlier timetables we have considered, but commonplace these days, is the emergence of dated alterations to train times on Saturday nights to take account of week-end engineering work, together with the appearance of the substitute BUS, prams (unfolded) and bicycles not conveyed.

There was only one Western Region train in or out of Weymouth on Sundays, and that late in the evening. The one and only to Weymouth did not call at Keynsham, passengers had to travel on the 20.18 Portsmouth service and change at Bath.

With the increased patronage of the station, inevitably, there was an increase in complaints. British Rail has a bad Press in Keynsham, sometimes deserved, sometimes not. There have been three principal sources of complaint: overcrowding, changes to the timetable and timekeeping. As we have just seen, overcrowding did regularly occur. During the morning peak trains arrived at Keynsham with all seats occupied, and for the return journey, trains left Temple Meads with passengers standing. But it only takes seven minutes between Keynsham and Bristol and what hardship does that entail compared with that with which Londoners have to contend every day? People regularly stand in boxes on four wheels (known as mini buses) but seem to rarely complain.

British Rail are not on such firm ground when considering changes to the timetable. It seems that every biannual change in the timetable gives cause for complaint. Trains disappear from the timetable, cease to call, or are radically re-timed. That sort of situation is endemic throughout BR and the reasons (or excuses) given are often not accepted by the public at their face value.

On the whole, timekeeping on trains calling at Keynsham is reasonable. Passengers are quick to complain if one particular train has a run of unpunctuality. More serious, is the impact of cancelled services due to shortage of stock or "staffing difficulties", often announced at short notice.

Press criticism is much reduced since the demise of the Keynsham Weekly Chronicle in 1992 which stirred the pot with readers' letters. One lady harked back to the day when there was a welcoming fire in the station waiting room! It had to be pointed out that even Badgerline, the local bus operator, did not provide such amenities.

For several years pressure had been put on British Rail to provide a public address system at Keynsham. In 1990 it appeared. The station is not situated in a heavily built up area, but British Rail had the volume turned up as if announcements were being made at Temple Meads, Bath, or wherever. A handful of local residents got together and in one inch high letters the local rag front page headline proclaimed "THE TRAIN NOW LEAVING TEMPLE MEADS IS RUINING OUR SLEEP." It was headline news on the local TV and they even got the local MP on to the act. It was incredible how so few people could create such an uproar in so short a time fanned, of course, by the media. BR over-reacted and turned the volume down to such a level that it is now inaudible to waiting passengers unless they are standing near to the speakers fixed to the under side of the footbridge: that is if the system is working, which is not very often.

Still in 1990, British Rail took space in the local Press to advertise "Be your Own Station Master." Keynsham was one of a number of stations included in the advertisement for this prestige appointment. There was at least one applicant and he got as far as obtaining planning permission for the provision of a portacabin in the station car park for the purpose of selling tickets, newspapers, coffee etc. The applicant was expected to provide his own portacabin and to arrange for the necessary main services. Considering the isolated position of the station, in relationship to the town, with little passing trade, and only a morning peak from 7.30 until 8.30, the project was a certain road to bankruptcy.

Then the Town Safety Group had the bright idea that it would be nice to have a public telephone box at the station — "because of its isolation, it is a frightening place for stranded

16. Station Masters

McDermott in his Official History of the Great Western Railway states "Station Master appointments dated from about 1860, although the term was often applied in earlier years." Previous to 1860, the person in charge at Keynsham was the station clerk.

There are some important features shown up in the list of clerks and station masters at Keynsham. Until 1940, all the appointees were under 40 years of age, many under 30. It was not until 1940 that long serving railwaymen were appointed to Keynsham, two of whom were short term appointments leading to retirement. Finally, Mr Bartrum was in post for 13 years until he was made redundant in 1965, co-incidental with the post being abolished.

From early census records and from the official records surviving at the Public Record Office at Kew, it can be seen how mobile railwaymen were in those early days, a period when most of the population were still decidedly prisoners to their own local environment. Many started work on the railway far from their home town or district. The mobility thus created appears to have had an unsettling influence, judging by the number of resignations at Keynsham in the early days, which were roughly in proportion to that of railwaymen in general during that period.

When the station opened on 31st August 1840, EDWARD STROUDWATER TAYLOR, a Londoner was already there, it being his first appointment, officially recorded as August 1840. He stayed until 1842, when he moved on to Bath as Chief Clerk. In June 1845 he was appointed to the booking office at Brimscombe, Stroud. On the face of it that appears to be a demotion. Perhaps it was, for in January 1858 he was "discharged" by the Reduction Committee. They even had economy purges back in 1858 but, of course, there was no redundancy money!

In the same month as Taylor moved on, December 1842, GEORGE NUGENT TYRELL arrived from Exeter, again a first appointment. He stayed until April 1845 when he returned to Exeter, the Bristol and Exeter Railway having already arrived there on 1st May 1844. Tyrell subsequently returned to the GWR and went on to become a railway celebrity. In 1864 he was appointed the first Superintendent of the Line, with responsibility for all passenger services. In status he was a Chief Officer. He stayed in the post until he retired in 1888 at the age of 72, McDermott referring to him as "The aged Superintendent of the Line." Whilst at Keynsham, Tyrell had at least one disciplinary matter to deal with. At a GWR Board Meeting held on 14th August 1843, it was minuted "Samuel Taylor, a porter at Keynsham, not appearing, was dismissed upon a Report of the Station Clerk against him." Taylor (a mere porter) had the doubtful honour of his case being dealt with at Board level.

Tyrell was replaced in the same month, April 1845, by GEORGE DINHAM, transferred from Maidenhead, where he had joined the railway in 1841. He remained at Keynsham until he resigned the railway service in 1852. The 1851 census records the Dinham family as under:

George	Married	Age	41	Born	St.Giles, Middlesex*	Railway Superintendent
Margaret	Daughter		12		Camberwell Surrey	Scholar
Jeanette	Daughter		10		Southwark Surrey	Scholar
Edward	Son		7		Maidenhead Berks	Scholar
Marina	Daughter		3		Keynsham	
Ann Bryant	House Servant		23		Keynsham	

* The GWR Staff Register shows him born at Camberwell.

Dinham evidently had grand ideas of his own importance for he was not a Railway Superintendent, but only a humble station clerk. It is interesting to note that his three eldest children were all classed as scholars in days long before schooling was compulsory. The absence of his wife from the census and the appearance of a house servant could mean that he was a widower.

Two others followed in relatively quick succession to Dinham. JOHN GEORGE INDERMOUR was at Keynsham from October 1852 until August 1856, when he moved on to Bruton. He had joined the railway at Exeter in 1847.

ROBERT FRENCH LAWRENCE joined the railway in the booking office at Bristol in February 1856, and by the following August he was at Keynsham. He resigned in January 1858.

JOHN BANFIELD OWERS (1858–1873) There was a gap of two months prior to the arrival of Owers in March 1858, as station clerk, for a reign of 15 years — the second longest stint. From his subsequent history he would appear to have been a bit of a character. He joined the GWR in the Accountant's Department at Wolverhampton and his age was recorded as 26, about which there was some doubt. That was in November 1855. The official record also showed him as deceased. There was also some doubt about that when somebody added a pencil question mark. He was very much alive when he arrived at Keynsham! He was officially appointed station master at Keynsham in November 1860 — without any increase in salary. The transition was one of nomenclature or status only.

The 1861 census records the family as under:

John Barfield Owers
    Age 25   Railway Station Master
Mary Ann Owers
    26   Wife
Ann Owers
    50   Widow

It will be noted that Owers was one year younger than when he joined the railway five years earlier! All three were born in Ilminster. By the date of the 1871 Census, Owers had promoted himself to "Accountant and Station Master"!

He resigned from the railway in April 1873. We now turn to the Bristol and Clifton Directory and find that in 1872 Mrs Owers Jnr was at the Wine and Spirit Vaults in Bath Street, Keynsham.[1] In the directories for 1876-78 John was also at the Wine and Spirit Vaults, now designated the Wingrove Hotel. Two years later he is shown as an Estate Agent! The 1881 Census affords some clarification as Owers described himself as a Wine Merchant and Estate Agent, still at the Wingrove Hotel in Bath Street. It would appear that his wife had died in the interim ten years between the Census records and, perhaps, also his mother whose name was not recorded. In lieu there appeared:

Portia J. Owers,
        his wife aged 33 born in Bath.
also
Mary A. Owers,
        his spinster sister, aged 45,
        born in Ilminster.

There is no record of any children born within either marriage.

The 1891 Census records that Owers had moved from the Wingrove Hotel to Manchester House in the High Street. Although still describing himself as an Estate Agent, Manchester House indicates that he was now in the drapery business, confirmed by the presence in the household of one Anne Arlett, aged 21 (place of birth unknown) who was described as a Draper's Assistant.

There is an obvious necessity to treat the recorded age of Owers and his wife with some reserve. Owers, when he joined the railway in 1855 was 26: by the date of the 1861 Census he was only 25: thirty years later, according to the 1891 Census he was 51. His wife, Portia, had only aged five years between 1881 and 1891, from 33 to 38!

Although Owers was Station Master from 1858 until 1873, there is the strange interlude of WILLIAM JOHN BROAD who is recorded

---

[1]*Bath Street is now Bristol Road*

127

as Station Master at Keynsham from July until November 1860, although he was only 20 at the time. Furthermore, he was not paid the going rate for the job. When he moved on in the November, that co-incided with the reclassification of Owers from Station Clerk to Station Master. All very strange.[2]

Following the resignation of Owers in April 1873 ROBERT JOHN NALDER was in office as Station Master for a matter of weeks, presumably until RICHARD BLACKBOROW (not Blackburn as in some Directories) was appointed the following month. Blackborow was born on 13th July 1848, joined the railway in November 1866. In the intervening 8½ years prior to his arrival at Keynsham he had served at five locations, viz Crumlin, Portskewett, Landore, Carmarthen Junction and Slough. After less than three years he moved on to become Station Master at Taplow, only four miles from Slough from whence he had come to Keynsham, He was still only 27 years of age.

There followed another short term appointment in the name of JOHN TEMPLETON NICOL, aged 24, who was Station Master from January until June 1876, at which date he was dismissed for some unspecified misdemeanour.

MARK GIBBONS, aged 25, arrived in June 1876 and stayed until April 1881. At the date of the 1881 Census the following particulars were recorded:

Mark Gibbons
Age   29
Born Warfield, Berks
Station Master
Jeannette Emily Gibbons
Age   28
Born St Johns Wood
Emily Edith
Age   5
Born Aylesbury
Scholar
Annie Rebecca
Age   1
Born Keynsham

Emma Williams
Age   17
Born Frome
House Servant

Gibbons resigned in April, very shortly after the decennial census had been taken.

There was a two month gap between the departure of Gibbons and the arrival of ARTHUR MARTIN. Possibly, Gibbons' resignation had been unexpected and the railway had to look around for a suitable replacement. Martin came from the Divisional Superintendent's Office at Bristol and returned there after a two year stint at Keynsham.

THOMAS WILLIAM BOHN stayed at Keynsham for ten years, from 1883 until 1893. He came from Witham where he had been Station Master for only ten months. From Keynsham, in January 1893 Bohn moved on to Warminster, again as Station Master, but only after fourteen months he found himself back at Witham. Sixteen months later, on 3rd July 1895, he was dismissed from the railway service. Witham was one of those delightful railway stations in the middle of nowhere, at a junction between the secondary Cheddar Valley and Weymouth lines. Therefore, it can be conjectured that Bohn was demoted back to Witham and probably dismissed from there for inefficiency.

Bohn is recorded in the 1891 Census as follows:

Thomas W. Bohn
Age   35
Born Croydon
Railway Agent
Deborah Bohn
Age   33
Born Chippenham
Harold Bohn
Age   6
Born Keynsham

Bohn was succeeded by JOHN RICHARD TAYLOR who was at Keynsham for the five years 1893 to 1898, when he moved on to be Station Master at Wootton Bassett. The next

[2]PRO Rail 394/146

three years saw three occupants in the post:

ARTHUR JOHN CAMPFIELD
April 1898 until May 1899
HARRY CHARLES CRADDOCK
May 1899 until June 1900
FRANK GEORGE DUNFORD
July 1900 until Mar 1901

Of the above, the first and last both moved on to be Station Masters at Maiden Newton. The other man lost his status as Station Master on transfer to Shepton Mallet, although regaining status in 1904 when appointed to Box.

We now turn to the tragic case of WILLIAM GARARD (1901–1903). He had only been in office for 18 months when his wife, Mrs Helen Georgina Garard committed suicide in the station house, not long after the birth of their child. The inquest was held on the following day, Saturday 4th October 1902 in the afternoon at Wilkins' Restaurant, Keynsham. The gory details are recorded in the issue of the Bath Chronicle dated 9th October.

Mr Garard was moved to Castle Cary as Station Master in March, 1903, although his successor had been appointed a month earlier. It seems that Gerard could not settle in his new post and he resigned from the railway service. The official record states "Paid to 12th July 1903". Overall, it would appear that the railway was a sympathetic and caring employer.

The Garard family were the last to live in the station house. Ultimately, the ground floor became a parcel office, the stairs to the upper floor were removed and a hole left in the ceiling at that point. In that condition the house remained until demolition in 1970. Not unexpectedly, the house was reputed to be haunted, but there is no substantive evidence. Maybe, those events were the reason which dictated the removal of the station administrative offices to the down platform a few years later.

SAMUEL PHILIP LAMBERT only stayed the three years from 1903 until 1906. He then moved on to be the Station Master at Langport West, which he must have found more congenial, for he stayed there until his retirement in 1936. Whilst in Keynsham, he lived at Springfield House. He was also the third man to arrive at Keynsham from Witham!

THOMAS GOODLAND WEBB (1906–1911) joined the railway on the passenger side at Shepton Mallet in 1891. Following short stints at Weymouth and Wells, he was appointed Chief Goods Clerk at Radstock (GW) in 1901. Five years later he became Station Master at Keynsham. On the testimony of his daughter, the railway wanted Webb to live in the station house, but he refused on the grounds that the bloodstains were still on the floor.

Whilst at Radstock GWR, Webb courted and married the daughter of Radstock's Somerset and Dorset Station Master. She was probably a Miss Caines.[3]

Webb had an interesting career after leaving Keynsham for a promotion to be the GWR Parcels Agent at Temple Meads. With the advent of war, he moved to be the Military Traffic Agent at Avonmouth, followed by a secondment to the military authorities as Traffic Manager at Bramley near Reading. Returning to the GWR after the war, he was appointed Outdoor Representative to the Bristol Divisional Superintendent. In 1928, he once more became Parcel Agent, by then a far more important post than the one he had previously occupied. His daughter used to tell the tale that her father would come home very pleased because he had won traffic from the LMS although a longer mileage was involved. In 1934 the competing railways saw sense, drawn by the need for economy, and Webb was appointed Parcels Agent at Bristol for both the GWR and LMS. By the time he retired on his 60th birthday, 30th March 1936, Webb was a widower. He married a second time when his bride was Miss D. Banks, who was the manageress of the Temple Meads Refreshment Rooms. He died on 8th February 1942 at the age of 65.

According to the Electoral Roll for 1912, Webb lived in Rock Road. Shortly afterwards he was at "Limefield", Chandag Road. That later became 2 Chandag Road with, today, the house name still carved into the stonework of the gatepost. By the mid-thirties he was at 49

[3]Radstock Coal and Steam, Chris Handley (Millstream Books 1991)

Bristol Road, now demolished, where he died.

1911 to 1965

We now move into a new era, from several points of view. The four station masters to be considered all ultimately retired, a complete contrast to all the preceding youngsters who all moved on. Two of the four were, indeed, short term appointments leading up to retirement. Three of the four probably retired on their 60th birthdays, which was the norm in those days. The relevant official GWR staff records at the Public Records Office (PRO), Kew, ceased between 1910 and 1915 with nothing official to replace them, as far as can be ascertained. Much that follows has been gathered from local sources, including press reports, where available.

HERBERT NELSON BLAIR (1911–1940) arrived from Penzance circa October 1911 where he was the parcels clerk. He stayed at Keynsham for no less than 29 years. It has not been possible to establish a firm date for his retirement, but without much doubt it was on his 60th birthday, 20th August 1940. He joined the railway in 1897 at Helston, serving also at St Ives, Redruth and Tavistock. There was at that time, a Mr W. Blair, station master at Penzance, possibly his father. Blair retired because of ill health in 1911, but survived until May 1940 to the great age of 86.

H.N. Blair first lived at 'Rosemont', Rock Road where, according to the Electoral Roll of 1913, his landlord was Charles Willcox. Two years later, Wright's Directory shows him at 'Egremont', Rock Road, presumably, that eventually became 38, Rock Road, of which he is described as the owner in the Electoral Roll of 1939. It must be assumed that he moved house in Rock Road, but the records which are available are unhelpful.

ALFRED BRICKNELL SPAREY (1940–1944) who followed Blair was already 56 when he was appointed to Keynsham. He was probably glad to settle down into a permanently based post, if even for only the last four years of his railway service. He had been a relief station master within the Bristol Division, with temporary postings as far away as Farringdon,

the other side of Swindon. There was a report in the GWR Magazine for May 1928 covering the death of Mr H.G. Greenaway, relief station master, who was buried in the Keynsham cemetery on 23rd March of that year, six station masters from local stations acting as bearers. Sparey was, undoubtedly, Greenaway's successor and, indeed, his family pointed to the year 1928 as the date of their father's appointment quite independent of the magazine report.

Sparey lived for many years at Hawthorn Villa which, in due course became 8, Chandag Road, only a few doors from his one time predecessor, Mr Webb.

Sparey joined the railway at Clevedon in 1900, but spent some of his early years in the Divisional Superintendent's Office at Temple Meads. He too, probably retired on his 60th birthday, 14th July 1944. He had a large family, some of whom still live in Keynsham.

PERCY BELL (1944–1952), a native of Norton St. Philip, arrived at Keynsham from Melksham in 1924, according to an extensive retirement report which appeared in the Keynsham Weekly Chronicle dated 10th May 1952. It is likely that he spent some of the 20 years prior to his appointment as Station Master in the Goods Department, and only in the later years did he become the senior booking office clerk, rather than his more grandiose chief booking office clerk. He certainly retired on his 60th birthday, 6th May 1952. At the date of his retirement he lived at 38, Charlton Road. Following his retirement he became the proprietor of a sweet shop in Totterdown, Bristol. He is remembered by the author as a somewhat gloomy man, more concerned about the value of his nationalised railway shares than anything else.

Finally, we come to NORMAN ROBERT BARTRUM (1952–1965) who joined the railway in 1915 in a clerical capacity at the rural station of Wylie at the age of 15. Wylie station was situated on the line between Warminster and Salisbury. At the end of 1926, following a number of intermediate postings, he moved from Pewsey to Cranmore, spending 17 years there, first as a clerk, then as Station Master. In 1943 he moved back to Pewsey as

Mr N.R. Bartrum, the last Station Master standing at the far Bath end of the up platform. Undated.

Courtesy Mrs A. Frere

Station Master and moved on to Keynsham a fortnight after the retirement of Bell. Bartrum went on beyond the normal retirement age of 60 as enjoyed by his predecessors. He would have liked to retire on his 65th birthday, but an unsympathetic management made him redundant five months previous in June 1965. He died in 1973. His son and two daughters still live in the town. By courtesy of his family,

a synopsis of Bartrum's railway career, as recorded in his own fair hand, is reproduced on page 132).

MISS NORA G. WEBB, the surviving booking clerk, stayed on at the station for a few more months, presumably to tidy up the paper work, and she officially retired in October 1965[4]. The running of the station was then left to the

---

[4]*Rail News December 1965.*

Miss Nora Webb – daughter of Mr T.G. Webb, Station Master at Keynsham 1906–11 – booking clerk at Keynsham and Somerdsle 1940–69. Photographed on 9th September 1977, eight years into her retirement.

Author

tender mercies of the two remaining porters — Ernie Hallett and 'Arry Stock. They, in turn, were made redundant when the station became unstaffed on 6th October 1969.

Miss Webb came from a railway family, her father was the Keynsham Station Master (1906–1911) and, as we have seen, her grandfather was at one time the Station Master at Radstock on the Somerset and Dorset. Miss Webb was originally employed at Temple Meads, but with war time travel problems she managed to get a transfer to Keynsham in 1940. After her colleague, Mr Watts, went over to the Goods Office in 1956 (see chapter 4) the early and late shifts in the Booking Office were continued for a time with a seemingly succession of temporary appointments. Miss Webb's final years at the station were on the basis of a single shift.

Ernie Hallett arrived at Keynsham from Castle Cary in 1931, appointed as a motor driver, but by 1949 he was working as a porter. 'Arry Stock was transferred from Saltford in 1948.

So, after nearly 130 years, Keynsham became an uncared for, unstaffed station, bereft of buildings and a frustrated British Rail who tried their very best to be rid of it altogether.

Station master Bartrum's hand written account of his railway career.

17. Personalities

On 13th September 1894, there was a small gathering in the back parlour of the Crown Inn, Bristol Road, to hear from visitors from Bedminster concerning the advantages to be gained from forming a local Co-operative Society. Following the meeting the locals extended the courtesy of escorting their visitors to the railway station for their homeward journey. Whilst waiting for the train, it was suggested that Mr T.R. Tucker should act as Treasurer and, so prompted, all six of the locals handed over one shilling each (5p), and thus, on Keynsham station the Keynsham Co-operative Society was born.[1] One of the six was Mr J.G. Harvey who had a newsagent's business in a small and ancient cottage in Station Road, now occupied by Family Books. Harvey sold his newspapers on the station platform each morning to the commuters of the day, whatever the weather. A picture of John Harvey and his wife, taken about 1904, outside their cottage, appears in a book of old photographs of Keynsham and Saltford, published by Barbara Lowe and Tony Brown. Conspicuous are the advertisements for the Bristol Daily Press. The newspaper business survived in Station Road and the last one in the family business and in residence (much improved since 1904) was a member of the Keynsham Urban District Council. Cllr Harvey died in June 1966.

In the Public Record Office at Kew[2] there is a schedule of uniformed staff employed at Keynsham station between 1898 and 1904. Its most remarkable feature is the mobility of the staff concerned. It would appear that the establishment was four signalmen, two porters and two lad porters. Over the six years concerned there were only two individuals out of the 25 who lasted out the whole of the period, i.e.

    R.Coombes   Porter
    F.C.Devenish   Signalman

Of the 18 who moved on, one was dismissed, but all the remainder were transferred to other locations within the Bristol Division. No fewer than seven lad porters were taken on, probably straight from school, five of whom had moved on by 1904.

Coombes and Devenish were destined to stay at Keynsham for many more years. Coombes retired in 1917, by which time he had graduated from porter to checker. He received as a retirement present from colleagues and local tradespeople a "handsome barometer, suitably inscribed", together with a smokers outfit. He started on the railway at Bristol in 1877 and spent 39 years at Keynsham.

Devenish was still a signalman at Keynsham when he retired in 1924 after 50 years service, of which 40 were spent at Keynsham. Mr J.M. Sheppard, the oldest season ticket holder, presided at the retirement proceedings and Devenish received a divan chair at the hands of Mr H.R. Griffiths, the Divisional Superintendent. It was normal practice in those days to have a personality to preside on such occasions, perhaps a season ticket holder, but often it was a local trader, sometimes the local vicar. Devenish must have been highly regarded for such an exalted personality as the Divisional Superintendent to travel out from Bristol to Keynsham to make the presentation.

Another feature of the retirement of local station staff was generous participation by passengers and local traders. For example, when Mr Redwood retired in 1922 after 20 years as station master at nearby Saltford, he received:

    A silver cigarette case and a box of cigarettes from the station staff
    A handsome inscribed chair from the farmers
    A bulky wallet of treasury notes from the local residents.

Saltford does not even have a station now.

---

[1] *A Study in Democracy: Being an Account of the Rise and Progress of Industrial Co-operation in Bristol.* Edward Jackson (CWS 1911)

[2] *RAIL 264/421.*

Reverting back to 1904, the following report appeared in the GWR Magazine for September:

"On August Bank Holiday, a little girl of about five years of age wandered to Londonderry Wharf and fell into the River Avon. Although there were a large number of holiday makers on the spot at the time no one offered to rescue the child. Lock-keeper White happening to pass was informed of the occurrence and without divesting himself of his heavy clothing, dived into the water and brought the child out, afterwards resuscitating it. He was rewarded by the Royal Humane Society."

White retired in 1921 when he too was presented with a suitably inscribed barometer by H.N. Blair, the station master, with Mr D. Stowell of the Canal Department in attendance. White had been the lock-keeper at Keynsham for 43 years. He died at Keynsham in 1930, aged 73.

To put that into perspective, the canalised River Avon between Bath and Hanham Lock was part of the Kennet and Avon Canal which the GWR purchased back in 1852 at a knock down price, the bottom having fallen out of the canal trade following the arrival of the railway. Hence, lock-keeper White was a railway employee and part of the Keynsham establishment.

Prior to 1939 there was a brisk trade in barometers as retirement gifts, with accompanying business for engravers. A social study of retirement proceedings in industry generally would make an interesting thesis for a PhD.

A colourful figure (in more senses than one) during the inter-war years was George Ollis, who was employed by the GWR as a sub-ganger at St Anne's Park. He was also Keynsham's Town Crier from 1910 until 1945. At the National Town Criers' Competition, held at Pewsey on 15th September 1926, he was awarded a prize for the second year in succession as the best dressed town crier. The report says "He looked particularly smart in his costume of green knee breeches, buckled shoes and three cornered hat. He was the only town crier to wear a wig". His outfit was described as in the characteristic style of the Tudor period.[3] He retired from the railway in 1946 and died in 1951.

There was a report in the Bath and Wilts Chronicle and Herald for 26th January 1935 concerning a Mr J. Allen, a native of Cornwall, who started work on the GWR at Keynsham at some unspecified date, who still lived in the town and was the Chairman of the Parish Council. At the date of the report he had just been appointed Station Master at Bath.

---

[3]*GWR Magazine November 1926. See also "Around Keynsham & Saltford in Old Photographs" Barbara Lowe & Tony Brown (Alan Sutton Publishing, 1988).*

18. 150 Years

On 31st August 1990, the line from Bristol to Bath, including Keynsham station, celebrated its 150th Anniversary. The Keynsham Local History Society and the Keynsham Civic Society banded together and approached British Rail, who, in response, provided some bunting for the occasion and a red carnation for every commuter, driver and guard of every train calling during the morning peak. (The carnations were of exceptional quality, for the author wore his as a guest at a wedding the next day). In keeping with the occasion, members of the two Societies were dressed in Victorian costume. The carnations disappeared into the button holes of the commuters and the bunting disappeared safely back into BR's keeping as soon as the last commuter had departed.

British Rail ran a commemorative train (of a sort) for the occasion, when the 12.15 HST from Bristol to Paddington conveyed the Lord Mayor of Bristol and the Mayor of Bath as far as Bath, where they and sundry officials went off for a celebratory lunch. Sadly, the local Societies failed to persuade British Rail to stop the train at Keynsham, or to be included in the junketing.

A group in period costume standing on the downside station steps, on 31st August 1990, to celebrate the 150th anniversary of the opening of the station.

Back row:	Helen Dunford, Tony Brown, Trevor Whitehead,
3rd row:	John Dunford, Dr Anderson, Margaret Whitehead,
2nd row:	John Hampton, Iris Lerpiniere,
Front row:	Barbara Lowe, Victoria Anderson, Penny Grant (age 6).

19. Postcript

Writing in 1996, very little has happened since the 150th "Celebrations" at Keynsham over which British Rail has had any control. Yet, outside influences have been of considerable moment.

Early in 1990 the Ministry of Defence (MOD) confirmed earlier rumours that there were proposals to relocate to Keynsham 3,800 personnel from London, Portsmouth and Portland. The favoured site was at Somerdale on land which was surplus to requirements and, therefore, adjacent to Keynsham station. The announcement was greeted with acclaim by the ruling party on the District Council, and, without any degree of surprise, by the local Chamber of Commerce. It was anticipated that a considerable passenger traffic would be attracted to Keynsham station.

Now, the road system at Keynsham is basically that prevailing when Keynsham was a village, although upgraded as far as possible to modern standards. There was immediate response from the local amenity societies who reacted with horror at the thought of a proposed car park for 2,500 cars and trying to accommodate them on a road system already heavily congested at peak times; they were vociferously supported by both the Keynsham and Saltford residents.

With no abatement in the opposition, the District Council passed the issue to Avon County Council. They being of a different political persuasion asked for a Public Enquiry. The MOD retired from the fray.

Somewhat late in the day a Development Company came up with a plan to accommodate the MOD on a site between Keynsham and Saltford adjacent to Pixash Lane. The site was to be provided with a private station, available to MOD personnel only, where British Rail would arrange for their InterCity trains and sprinters to call. Whether BR had been consulted was not made clear; it should be viewed as a doubtful starter. When the MOD learnt that some of the proposed site was on green belt land they did not want to know.

Although the MOD insisted that Keynsham had always been the preferred site, they did have an alternative in mind in North Bristol, not far from the then Filton station and only a mile or two from Bristol Parkway station where frequent InterCity trains are available to London, South Wales, the Midlands and the North and West of England.

The displaced Filton station was a run down basic two platform affair unloved by both British Rail and the public alike. A new station, Filton Abbey Wood was constructed some 300 yards nearer Bristol and opened on 11th March 1996. The station is adjacent to the new MOD office complex. According to newspaper reports: the station was constructed at a cost of £1½ million, financed by the Ministry of Transport, the MOD, local authorities, businesses and Regional Railways South Wales and West.

At Bath, where there is a significant MOD presence, many of whom are being transferred to Filton, the County Council have intended to provide a new Park and Ride station at Newbridge on the extreme western extremity of the City and west of Twerton tunnel. At the time of writing, and with the demise of the County of Avon, the future of that proposal is unknown. Irrespective of that proposal, a new Bath to Filton service has been provided with additional trains calling at Keynsham.

A more serious threat to the well being of Keynsham station emerged in 1993/4. The City Fathers in Bristol had been active for some time in seeking a solution to the chronic traffic chaos in the City Centre and one development was the provision of a Park and Ride facility at Brislington, right on the eastern boundary to the City limits and only two miles from the Keynsham High Street. That extracted some customers from Keynsham station when it opened towards the end of 1993. Worse was to come a few months later, in early 1994, when the southern section of the Bristol Ring Road was opened linking Longwell Green with Hicks Gate and the Park and Ride only a mile or so up the road. The effect was immediate, motorists abandoned the railway and the car park occupancy down to a mere half a dozen vehicles. The Park and Ride and the Ring Road between them have decimated the station patronage. However, there is a small trickle

Cl. 153308 at Keynsham on the 10.33 Bristol to Southampton, 19th July 1996. These trains are single car rebuilds of the Cl. 155s (see p125).   *Author*

HST 253 019 in original livery on a Bristol to Paddington express on 20th March 1977. The lifted former paper mill siding is on the left. The notice-board reads "All trains must stop dead here"!   *Author*

back to the train caused, no doubt, by that same traffic chaos already referred to. In the evening peak, the Park and Ride buses can sometimes be seen in convoy, London Transport fashion, and the timetable in shreds.

Turning to the accompanying timetable for the Winter of 1995/6, it is completely different from any of those we have previously looked at. The old order has vanished: the last heritage dmus finished at the end of the 1992 summer service. The locomotive hauled trains to Portsmouth were superseded even earlier, back in 1988. In lieu, there is a series of modern dmus in service ranging from the four wheeled Cl. 143s, up through the 150/2s and 153s to the top of the range Cl. 158s on prestige routes. The whole fleet is concentrated on Cardiff Canton for maintenance purposes and is available for work in the whole of the West of England, South Wales, including the Valleys and the Marches. In short, the whole of the rolling stock attributed to Regional Railways South Wales and West is based on Cardiff Canton.

So having set the scene for Keynsham, the Cl. 158s work the Portsmouth line, the 150/2s the Weymouth and Southampton services, with the 143s and 153s appearing on the purely local trains into the Westbury area. At last, Keynsham has a decent train service to Weymouth. Locomotive hauled trains would have completely vanished but for the shortage of dmu rolling stock. Thus, the 16.33 from Bristol (Keynsham at 16.40), although rostered for a 150/2, is more frequently provided with a Cl. 37/4 with renovated coaches hired from the preservation centre at Carnforth.

Until the Summer of 1995 the 37/4 was provided by Crewe. Since then Cardiff have gathered in their 37411/2/3 from St Blazey and have acquired 37427 from Motherwell, still sporting its Regional Railways Scotrail livery.

The full roster for the duty is:

06.59	Westbury to Weymouth	
08.40	Weymouth to Bristol (not calling at Keynsham)	
16.33	Bristol to Weymouth	FSX
19.38	Weymouth to Westbury	FSX

On Fridays the locomotive and coaches go over to Cardiff at 11.30, from Bristol to work the 16.45 to Manchester, returning empty to Crewe for the 21.38 back to Cardiff. Meanwhile, the 16.33 roster is taken over by a 150/2 on Fridays and Saturdays.

As to the actual timetable at Keynsham it will be noted that on the main London line there are only two trains to Swindon in the up direction and none in the down. Those are no more than positional movements by the operating department. The one time lavish service to Chippenham and Swindon is no more for the simple reason that all the intermediate stations are no more; they were chopped with the Beeching Axe. InterCity now serve the two centres with their HST Shuttle.

We now see, once again, trains turning around at Bath, including one at 15.08 SX from Penzance, returning to Paignton at 16.01 SX. On the other hand the first train of the day from Bath, the early 05.29, or thereabouts, has disappeared.

Apart from the midday train to Brighton, the only Portsmouth line services that call at Keynsham on week-days are one in the early morning and two in the evening. The new regime sometimes has trains to or from exotic stations, such as the train from Brighton calling at 12.10 which goes through to Tenby. The train calling at 07.55 starts from Frome on Saturdays and goes through to Carmarthen, but for the rest of the week it commences its journey at Exmouth.

Winter Services at Keynsham 1995-6

Up Trains Rostered for	From	Time at Keynsham	To
WEEKDAYS			
158	Cardiff	06.02 SX	Portsmouth Harbour
158 + 150/2	Cardiff	07.10 SO	Portsmouth Harbour & Weymouth
150/2	Bristol	07.39 SX	Southampton (from Filton* from 11th March)
158	Bristol	08.00 SX	Bath
150/2	Bristol	08.40 SX	Weymouth
158	Bristol	09.08 SX	Bath
150/2	Bristol	09.40	Weymouth
150/2	Bristol	10.40	Southampton
150/2	Bristol	12.05	Weymouth
158	Cardiff	13.05	Brighton
150/2	Bristol	13.40	Southampton
150/2	Bristol	14.40	Weymouth
158	Penzance	15.08 SX	Bath
150/2	Bristol	15.40 SO	Southampton
158	Paignton	16.02 SX	Swindon
150/2 or 37/4	Bristol	16.40	Weymouth
143 or 153	Weston-super-Mare	16.57 SX	Bath
143 or 153	Filton*	17.08 SX	Westbury (not calling Bristol TM)
150/2	Bristol	17.40	Weymouth
153	Bristol Parkway	17.55 SX	Swindon (not calling Bristol TM)
150/2	Weston-super-Mare	18.10 SX	Warminster
150/2	Bristol	18.40	Westbury
143	Weston-super-Mare	19.10 SX	Bath
158	Cardiff	19.29	Portsmouth Harbour
143	Bristol	19.59 SX	Bath
150/2	Bristol	20.40	Weymouth
158	Cardiff	21.40	Portsmouth Harbour
158	Cardiff	22.47 SX	Frome
158	Cardiff	23.17 SO (s)	Warminster
158	Cardiff	23.47 SX (s)	Westbury

Winter Services at Keynsham 1995-6

Up Trains

Rostered for	From	Time at Keynsham	To
SUNDAYS			
158	Cardiff	09.12	Portsmouth Harbour
158 x 2	Cardiff	10.55	Portsmouth Harbour & Brighton
158 x 2	Cardiff	11.55	Portsmouth Harbour & Brighton
150/2	Bristol	12.55	Southampton
158	Bristol	16.25	Portsmouth Harbour
158	Cardiff	18.00	Weymouth
158	Cardiff	18.41	Portsmouth Harbour
150/2	Cardiff	20.40	Weymouth
158	Cardiff	23.52 (s)	Warminster

Down Trains

Rostered for	From	Time at Keynsham	To
WEEKDAYS			
143 or 153	Bath	06.32 SX	Weston-super-Mare
143	Westbury	06.53 SX	Bristol (to Filton* from 11th March)
143	Westbury	07.11 SO	Bristol
158	Salisbury	07.31 SX	Cardiff (from Portsmouth Harbour MO)
153	Frome	07.55 SO	Carmarthen
150/2	Weymouth	07.56 SX	Bristol
143	Westbury	08.06 SX	Filton* (not calling Bristol TM)
158	Bath	08.26 SX	Bristol
158	Portsmouth Harbour	08.35 SO	Cardiff
150/2	Weymouth	08.59	Bristol
150/2	Southampton	10.12	Bristol
150/2	Southampton	11.10	Bristol
158	Brighton	12.10	Tenby
150/2	Weymouth	13.04	Bristol
150/2	Southampton	14.13	Bristol (from Westbury SO)
150/2	Weymouth	15.11	Bristol
158	Bath	16.01 SX	Paignton

Winter Services at Keynsham 1995-6

Down Trains Rostered for	From	Time at Keynsham	To
WEEKDAYS			
150/2	Weymouth	17.03	Bristol
158	Portsmouth Harbour	17.37 SO	Cardiff
143 or 153	Bath	17.59 SX	Keynsham (to Filton* from 11th March not calling Bristol TM)
158	Portsmouth Harbour	18.36	Cardiff
150/2	Weymouth	19.32	Bristol
158	Brighton	20.13	Cardiff
143, 150/2 or 153	Westbury	21.08	Cardiff
158	Portsmouth Harbour	22.51	Cardiff
SUNDAYS			
	Frome	10.21	Cardiff
158	Portsmouth Harbour	11.32	Cardiff
158	Brighton	14.35	Cardiff
150/2	Weymouth	17.04	Cardiff
150/2	Southampton	18.13	Cardiff
150/2	Weymouth	18.26	Bristol
158	Brighton	19.12	Cardiff
158	Brighton	20.09	Cardiff
150/2	Weymouth	21.24	Bristol
158	Portsmouth Harbour	22.31	Cardiff

Note: Minor differences to Saturday times have been ignored.

*For Filton, read Filton Abbey Wood when the replacement station opened on 11th March 1996.

(s) Set down only.

APPENDIX A

Excursions to Keynsham and Somerdale 1938 and 1939
Handbill Detail

Date	Point of origin	Fare Adult	Child	K & S arr	TM dpt	Refreshments if shown	Other
1938							
27 Jun	Principal stations						
	Plymouth North Road to Taunton	9/3	5/4½	2.20	9.05		On the return journey the train will be extended to Millbay, arr 1.0 ngt where buses will meet the train
28 Jun	Morecambe and Lancaster only	17/3 16/9	9/5 9/2	2.10	7.45		
24 May 26 Jun 21 Aug 18 Sep	Paddington and stations to Reading	8/3 6/9	4/11 4/2	1.45	7.35	Lunch 2/9 & 3/4 Supper "	
13 Jun 7 Sep	Portsmouth & Southsea stations to Fareham	7/3	4/5	1.44	6.55	Luncheon 2/6 Supper 2/6	
19 Jul	Ore, Hastings and most stations to Chichester	11/6 7/9	6/6 4/8	1.44	6.55	Luncheon 2/6 Supper 2/6	
15 Aug	Burnley, Accrington, Ramsbottom, Bury, Rochdale, Preston Blackburn, Darwen, etc to Stockport	14/6 12/6	8/- 7/-	2.08	6.35	Lunch and Supper incl. gratuities 5/6	

Date	Point of origin	Fare Adult	Child	K & S arr	TM dpt	Refreshments if shown	Other
17 Aug	Higham Ferrers, Wellingborough, stns to Leicester and Hinckley	9/3 8/3	5/6 5/-	2.18	8.20	Lunch and Supper incl. gratuities 5/6	Arrive Leicester 12 midnight
1939							
4 May	Sheffield Derby	11/- 8/9	6/3 5/2	2.20	8.20	Buffet: Ham, Beef, Tongue Sandwich 4d Poached egg on toast 8d Tea, coffee 3d	Special buses at Sheffield 6d or 3d Tickets to be purchased with rail tickets
18 May	Reading and stations to Wantage Road	6/9 5/8	4/2 3/7	2.20	7.35	No catering	
18 May	Brentford, Wimbledon Twickenham & stations to Wokingham	8/3 7/3	4/11 4/5	2.20	7.35	No catering	Change stations at Reading both directions
Daily 6 Jun 26 Sep	Weston-super-Mare	4/2	2/10	2.56	Any train		
6 Jun	Witney and stations to Oxford and Appleford Halt	7/- 6/3	4/3 3/11	1.45	7.35	Lunch 2/9 Supper 3/4	
7 Jun	Lincoln & stations to Newark and Nottingham	11/6 11/- 9/9	6/6 6/3 5/7½	2.42	8.20	Lunch 2/9 Supper 3/4	Corporation buses from Nottingham 6d and 3d
9 Jun	Local stations Cornwood to Bridgwater Stations Barnstaple to Norton Fitzwarren	8/9 5/3 7/9 5/9	5/1½ 3/4½ 4/7½ 3/7½	2.10	7.10		Arrive Cornwood 12.35am Corporation buses meet the train at Exeter St Davids Barnstaple line change Norton Fitzwarren both directions.

Date	Point of origin	Fare Adult	Fare Child	K & S arr	TM dpt	Refreshments if shown	Other
20 Jun	Stations Swanwick to Romsey	7/3 6/3	4/5 3/11	1.44	6.55	Lunch 2/6 Supper 2/6	
23 Aug	Coventry, Wolverhampton stations to B'ham New St	7/9 7/3	4/8 4/5	2.00	8.20	Lunch & Supper incl. Gratuities 5/6	
29 Aug	Bournemouth and stns. to Salisbury	6/9 4/8	4/2 3/1	1.44	6.55	Lunch 2/6 Supper 2/6	
31 Aug	Weymouth and stations to Westbury	6/3 4/8	3/11 3/1	1.45	6.55		

NOTES

1. Fares from intermediate calling stations are not shown here.
2. In some cases, a part of the journey from the home station was by a connecting timetabled service.
3. The difference between the railway's half-price child fare and the fare charged is always 9d or 9½d, i.e. the cost of Fry's standard 9d tea, with the halfpenny rounded off by the railway.
4. For decimal coversion see Appendix F.

144

APPENDIX B

Bitton railway Company Limited — Excursion Programme

Date	Restored Railway Destination	Fare £	Other Destinations	Fare £
1. BITTON YORKSHIREMAN 13 Oct 79	North Yorkshire Moors Railway (coach from Malton)	6.95	York Scarborough	4.20 4.20
2. BITTON CAMBRIAN 10 Aug 80	Talyllyn Railway	7.25	Fairbourne Barmouth	5.75 5.75
3. BITTON YORKSHIREMAN 11 Oct 80	North Yorkshire Moors Railway (coach from Malton)	7.95	York Scarborough	6.50 6.50
4. BITTON LAKES EXPRESS 4 May 81	Steamtown (Carnforth) & Lakeside & Haverthwaite Rly (coach from Carnforth)	10.50	Steamtown only Grange over Sands Coach tour of the Lake District	8.50 7.50 10.25
5. BITTON CORNISHMAN 16 Aug 81	Lappa Valley Railway (coach from Newquay)	8.25	Plymouth Looe Newquay	6.00 6.50 6.50
6. BITTON EAST ANGLIAN 17 Oct 81	North Norfolk Railway (coach from Norwich)	8.95	Cambridge Ely Thetford Norwich	6.45 6.45 6.45 6.95
7. BITTON PENNINE EXPRESS 1 May 82	Keighley & Worth Valley Rly Keighley & Worth Valley Rly and Yorkshire Dales Railway (coach from Keighley)	9.45 11.45	Skipton Carlisle Coach tour from Garsdale	8.25 8.95 10.45

145

Date	Restored Railway Destination	Fare £	Other Destinations	Fare £
8. **BITTON NORTH EASTERN** 9 Oct 82	North Yorkshire Moors Railway (coach from York)	11.45	York Castle Howard Durham Beamish Newcastle	7.45 10.95 8.45 10.95 9.45
9. **BITTON BELLE** 30 Apr 83	Bluebell Railway (double deck bus from Haywards Heath)	12.45	Brighton Coach tour to Arundel	7.50 9.45
10. **BITTON POACHER** 8 Oct 83	Nene Valley Railway (charter train to Orton Mere)	10.50	Peterborough Grantham Lincoln (St Marks) Coach tour from Grantham to Belvoir Castle	8.45 8.45 8.45 10.75
11. **BITTON PENNINE EXPRESS** 5 May 84	Keighley & Worth Valley Railway Keighley & Worth Valley Railway and Yorkshire Dales Railway (coach from Keighley)	10.75	Skipton Carlisle Coach tour from Garsdale	9.00 10.00 11.25
12. **BITTON THANET EXPRESS** 6 Oct 84	Kent and East Sussex Railway (coach from Ashford) or Romney Hythe & Dymchurch Rly (coach from Ashford)	12.00 13.25	Ashford Canterbury Coach tour to Leeds Castle	8.00 8.00 12.45
13. **BITTON CONWY EXPRESS** 4 May 85	Ffestiniog Railway or Snowdon Mountain Railway (coach from Llandudno Junc.)	14.00 15.00	Chester Llandudno Blaenau Ffestiniog Llechwedd Slate Caverns Coach tour of Snowdonia	9.50 10.50 11.00 14.00 12.00

Date	Restored Railway Destination	Fare £	Other Destinations	Fare £
14. **BITTON CONWY EXPRESS** 1 June 85	Repeat of No 13 above at the same fares.			
15. **BITTON YORKSHIREMAN** 5 Oct 85	North Yorkshire Moors Railway (coach from Malton)	5.50	York Scarborough	10.00 11.00
16. **BITTON LAKES EXPRESS** 10 May 86	Steamtown (Carnforth) & Lakeside & Haverthwaite Rly	18.00	Steamtown only Grange over Sands Coach tour of the Lake District	14.50 14.00 16.50

NOTES

1. All excursions were on Saturdays, except 2 and 5 which were on Sundays, and 4 which was on Bank Holiday Monday.

2. The first three trains started at Taunton and travelled to Bristol via Weston-super-Mare. There were connecting services from the Westbury line at Bristol.

3. There was no connecting service off the Westbury line for excursion No 5, it being a 7.45 departure from Bristol on a Sunday morning.

4. All other trains travelled to Bristol via Westbury, calling at all stations en route, including Keynsham, except Avoncliff and Freshford. Patronage at Keynsham was invariably good.

5. The fares quoted are from Keynsham (except No 5) and included admission to restored railway establishments and, where appropriate, a return trip on the railway concerned.

6. Two further excursions were organised. On 22nd November to Derby and the Midland Railway Trust at Butterley. Also to Nottingham and a coach tour of the Peak District. On 9th May 1987 there was an ambitious excursion to Edinburgh and supporting destinations. Both were cancelled due to lack of patronage, one of the factors being the escalating charges demanded by British Rail for train hire. The proposed fare to Derby in November 1986 was £13.75, whereas six months earlier it was only another 25p to go all the way to Grange-over-Sands.

APPENDIX C

1. Revenue Statistics — Keynsham 1907-1924

	PASSENGER*	INCOME GOODS	TOTAL	+	−
	£	£	£		
1907	4454	5710	10164		
1908	5044	4977	10021		143
1909	4912	5101	10013		8
1910	4970	4863	9833		180
1911	5274	4440	9714		119
1912	4998	4833	9831	117	
1913	5066	5287	10353	522	
1914	5590	5055	10645	292	
1915	5715	5936	11651	1006	
1916	5686	6412	12098	447	
1917	6681	7736	14417	1419	
1918	7780	7983	15763	1746	
1919	10194	8380	18574	2811	
1920	11247	18695	29942	11368	
1921	8317	14618	22935		7007
1922	8081	15210	23291	356	
1923	6755	11454	18209		5082
1924	6133	10735	16868		1341

*Includes parcel traffic

2. Revenue Statistics — Keynsham 1925-1939

	PASSENGER	INCOME GOODS	TOTAL	+	–
	£	£	£		
1925	5899	14241	20140	3272	
1926	5459	18157	23616	3476	
1927	5672	24591	30263	6647	
1928	6219	29515	35734	5471	
1929	5561	41833	47394	11660	
1930	5867	55619	61486	14092	
1931	5630	53327	58957		2529
1932	5432	48058	53490		5467
1933	5696	46928	52624		866
1934	5505	49732	55237	2613	
1935	5039	49481	54520		717
1936	4968	56647	61615	7695	
1937	5269	57392	62661	1046	
1938	5328	53500	58828		3833
1939	5611	58972	64583	5755	
			741,148		

APPENDIX D

1. Traffic Statistics – Keynsham Passenger 1925-1959

	Passenger		Season Tickets		Parcels			Lavatories			Misc	Total Coaching Stock receipts
	Number	£	Season Tickets	£	Rec'd	Dispatched	£	£	s	d	£	
1925	102046	3947	1420	1234	5899	4728	542			3	173	5899
1926	88863	3481	2088	1196	5853	4537	560			3	219	5459
1927	100035	3597	2521	1206	6877	5301	694			3	172	5672
1928	94218	3541	2255	1277	7166	6221	924			3	474	6219
1929	89198	3325	2044	1178	7045	6481	870			3	185	5561
1930	87511	3125	2707	1139	7919	8766	1440			2	161	5867
1931	82699	2696	2349	1000	8308	11029	1578			2	354	5630
1932	78694	2621	2310	950	9105	11674	1489			2	370	5432
1933	87456	3226	2526	934	11645	8421	1166			2	368	5696
1934	87901	3274	2532	936	12748	6904	1023			2	270	5505
1935	89055	3320	2287	834	12114	6941	611	1	9	1	273	5039
1936	86581	3267	2543	913	12535	5260	514	1	5	10	273	4968
1937	82541	3432	2648	987	12884	6019	583			2	265	5269
1938	76498	3499	2831	1020	12864	8672	650			1	158	5328
1939	78319	3380	3546	1198	14108	6455	654			5	374	5611
1940	87623	3922	3655	1289	13054	6862	809			5	396	6421
1941	125798	5842	4387	1320			526			11	107	7806
1942	88504	5873	3955	1490			1208			10	40	8621
1943	94655	8164	4432	1763			1279			8	82	11296
1944	85579	7403	3856	1631			1544			11	81	10670
1945	73147	7425	3060	1519			1027			4	–	9975
1946	56407	6011	2798	1554			662			6	47	8280
1947	55383	4763	2309	1584			608			2	52	7009
1948	44541	4507	1542	1274			734			1	39	6555
1949	58702	4093	1228	1304			1048			1	44	6490
1950	61659	3900	1002	1046			1303			3	43	6295
1951	66456	4064	932	916			1420			1	100	6501
1952	57226	3601	820	976	11342	5815	1380			2	43	6002
1953	59181	3739	644	824	14750	5835	1569			4	31	6167
1954	67027	4195	640	891	14927	6638	1722			4	25	6837
1955	57736	4448	649	874	16737	6858	2032			5	61	7420
1956	55197	4421	580	871	19110	8374	2753			7	425	8477
1957	68012	5556	690	801	21004	7112	2183			2	73	8615
1958	61367	4984	612	785	20241	6478	1877			3	23	7672
1959	60564	5466	496	839	21674	6328	1660			5	11	7981

2. Traffic Statistics – Keynsham Goods 1925-1949

Year	Coal & Coke Tons	Other Minerals Classes 1 to 6 Tons		General Merchandise Classes 7 to 21 Carted Tons		General Merchandise Classes 7 to 21 Non Carted Tons		Grand Total Tonnage	Livestock Number of Wagons
		Fwd	Rec'd	Fwd	Rec'd	Fwd	Rec'd		
1925	8749	2762	1271	2650	977	2181	1755	20345	412
1926	7163	2772	6297	2532	1386	2281	3094	25525	443
1927	9185	3334	2519	2717	1656	3350	7548	30309	477
1928	9132	3498	2180	5559	3232	4783	5623	34007	493
1929	10022	2263	621	5834	3890	12894	13574	49098	489
1930	11157	2755	1649	8216	7627	15858	10456	57718	371
1931	12121	1724	2836	6754	8307	13942	14452	60136	294
1932	12156	1264	2399	6926	10205	13532	12860	59342	181
1933	16639	1059	3240	6623	10658	13119	15667	67005	135
1934	22121	1304	1262	6294	6590	14143	19292	71006	165
1935	24972	1904	732	6819	7932	15876	21496	79731	217
1936	27502	2647	1274	6973	7488	17907	28963	92754	244
1937	28260	2517	1021	6771	7602	18993	32070	97234	288
1938	27627	2118	1000	5754	9095	16604	28618	90816	154
1939	29057	939	886	6611	6967	19183	32287	95930	261
1940	31591	1130	774	24940	30468	26081	62822	177806	115

Year	Coal & Coke Tons	Other Minerals Classes 1 to 6 Tons		General Merchandise Classes 7 to 21 Tons		Grand Total Tonnage	Livestock Number of Wagons
		Fwd	Rec'd	Fwd	Rec'd		
1941	27486	1896	1081	27077	37916	95456	255
1942	30418	2449	806	28324	32393	94390	235
1943	21458	2166	407	31751	41372	97154	172
1944	23593	1502	2129	34423	38836	99983	366
1945	21653	726	1097	35522	24469	83467	424
1946	23314	1944	655	23181	27957	77101	404
1947	20212	1759	1145	22450	30462	76058	437
1948	18687	1720	505	17271	25461	63644	152
1949	20885	1048	753	22227	33623	78536	267
Total 1925-49	495160					1,874,551	

APPENDIX E
Keynsham Station Masters

PRO Ref Rail 264	Name	Date of birth	Age	Appointment from	to	Previous Appointment	Next Appointment
2/46	TAYLOR Edward Stroudwater	Not Recorded	36	Aug 40	Dec 42	First Appointment	Chief Clerk Bath
2/42	TYRELL George Nugent	13.4.16	26	Dec 42	Apr 45	First Appointment	Exeter
403/49	DINHAM George	Not Recorded	35	Apr 45	Oct 52	Maidenhead	Resigned
401/33	INDEMCUR John George	Not Recorded	34	Oct 52	Aug 56	Booking Office Bath	Booking Office Bruton
401/155	LAWRENCE Robert French	Not Recorded	20	Aug 56	Jan 58	Booking Office Bristol	Resigned
399/58	OWERS John Banfield	8.32*	25*	Mar 58	Apr 73	Accountants Wolverhampton	Resigned
6/298	NALDER Robert John	4.9.34	38	Apr 73	May 73	DSO Bristol	DSO Bristol
399/274	BLACKBOROW Richard	13.7.48	24	May 73	Jan 76	Slough	SM Taplow
399/224	NICOL John Templeton	24.12.51	24	Jan 76	May 76	Taplow	Dismissed
399/241	GIBBONS Mark	20.11.50	25	Jun 76	Apr 81	Passenger Aylesbury	Resigned
399/440	MARTIN Arthur	26.2.54	27	Jun 81	Jan 83	DSO Bristol	DSO Bristol
399/676	BOHN Thomas William	11.55	27	Jan 83	Jan 93	SM Witham	SM Warminster
7/83	TUCKER John Richard	7.12.61	31	Jan 93	Apr 98	Passenger Shepton Mallet	SM Wootton Bassett

PRO Ref Rail 264	Name	Date of birth	Age	Appointment from	to	Previous Appointment	Next Appointment
7/373	CAMPFIELD Arthur John	18.1.67	31	Apr 98	May 99	Passenger Teignmouth	SM Maiden Newton
7/119	CHADDOCK Harry Charles	3.2.63	36	May99	Jun 00	Passenger Radstock	Passenger Shepton Mallet
7/491	DUNFORD Frank George	17.6.68	32	Jul 00	Mar 01	SM Witham	SM Maiden Newton
7/464	GARARD William	16.12.67	33	Mar 01	Mar 03	Passenger Weymouth	SM Castle Cary
7/614	LAMBERT Samuel Philip	30.8.67	35	Feb 03	Mar 05	SM Witham	SM Langport West
8/134	WEBB Thomas Goodland	30.3.76	30	Aug 06	Nov 11[+]	Radstock Goods	Parcels Agent Bristol TM
8/340	BLAIR Herbert Nelson	20. 8.80	31	Nov 11[+]	Aug 40[+]	Parcels Clerk Penzance	Retired
8/698	SPAREY Alfred Bricknell	14.7.84	56	Aug 40[+]	Jul144[+]	Relief SM	Retired
	BELL Percy	6.5.92	52	Jul 44[+]	May 52	Passenger Keynsham	Retired
	BARTRUM Norman Robert	27.11.00	51	May 52	Jun 65	SM Pewsey	Redundant

Notes

* Owers date of birth is uncertain

[+] these are the probable months in 1911, 1940 and 1944

SM = Station Master

DSO = Divisional Superintendent's Office

Passenger indicates booking office, parcels office or other passenger station duties

Blair and Sparey probably retired on their 60th birthdays.

APPENDIX F
Banking and Accounting conversion table

Old £sd	New £p	Old £sd	New £p	Old £sd	New £p	Old £sd	New £p	Old £sd	New £p	Old £sd	New £p	Old £sd	New £p	Old £sd	New £p	Old £sd	New £p	Old £sd	New £p
1	—	2/-	10	4/-	20	6/-	30	8/-	40	10/-	50	12/-	60	14/-	70	16/-	80	18/-	90
2	1	2/1	10	4/1	20	6/1	30	8/1	40	10/1	50	12/1	60	14/1	70	16/1	80	18/1	90
3	1	2/2	11	4/2	21	6/2	31	8/2	41	10/2	51	12/2	61	14/2	71	16/2	81	18/2	91
4	2	2/3	11	4/3	21	6/3	31	8/3	41	10/3	51	12/3	61	14/3	71	16/3	81	18/3	91
5	2	2/4	12	4/4	22	6/4	32	8/4	42	10/4	52	12/4	62	14/4	72	16/4	82	18/4	92
		2/5	12	4/5	22	6/5	32	8/5	42	10/5	52	12/5	62	14/5	72	16/5	82	18/5	92
6	3	2/6	13	4/6	23	6/6	33	8/6	43	10/6	53	12/6	63	14/6	73	16/6	83	18/6	93
7	3	2/7	13	4/7	23	6/7	33	8/7	43	10/7	53	12/7	63	14/7	73	16/7	83	18/7	93
8	3	2/8	13	4/8	23	6/8	33	8/8	43	10/8	53	12/8	63	14/8	73	16/8	83	18/8	93
9	4	2/9	14	4/9	24	6/9	34	8/9	44	10/9	54	12/9	64	14/9	74	16/9	84	18/9	94
10	4	2/10	14	4/10	24	6/10	34	8/10	44	10/10	54	12/10	64	14/10	74	16/10	84	18/10	94
11	5	2/11	15	4/11	25	6/11	35	8/11	45	10/11	55	12/11	65	14/11	75	16/11	85	18/11	95
1/-	5	3/-	15	5/-	25	7/-	35	9/-	45	11/-	55	13/-	65	15/-	75	17/-	85	19/-	95
1/1	5	3/1	15	5/1	25	7/1	35	9/1	45	11/1	55	13/1	65	15/1	75	17/1	85	19/1	95
1/2	6	3/2	16	5/2	26	7/2	36	9/2	46	11/2	56	13/2	66	15/2	76	17/2	86	19/2	96
1/3	6	3/3	16	5/3	26	7/3	36	9/3	46	11/3	56	13/3	66	15/3	76	17/3	86	19/3	96
1/4	7	3/4	17	5/4	27	7/4	37	9/4	47	11/4	57	13/4	67	15/4	77	17/4	87	19/4	97
1/5	7	3/5	17	5/5	27	7/5	37	9/5	47	11/5	57	13/5	67	15/5	77	17/5	87	19/5	97
1/6	7	3/6	17	5/6	27	7/6	37	9/6	47	11/6	57	13/6	67	15/6	77	17/6	87	19/6	97
1/7	8	3/7	18	5/7	28	7/7	38	9/7	48	11/7	58	13/7	68	15/7	78	17/7	88	19/7	98
1/8	8	3/8	18	5/8	28	7/8	38	9/8	48	11/8	58	13/8	68	15/8	78	17/8	88	19/8	98
1/9	9	3/9	19	5/9	29	7/9	39	9/9	49	11/9	59	13/9	69	15/9	79	17/9	89	19/9	99
1/10	9	3/10	19	5/10	29	7/10	39	9/10	49	11/10	59	13/10	69	15/10	79	17/10	89	19/10	99
1/11	10	3/11	20	5/11	30	7/11	40	9/11	50	11/11	60	13/11	70	15/11	80	17/11	90	19/11	£1

In order to be historically correct pre-decimalisation fares have been shown in accordance with what was normal every day practice, eg. 3/11 not 3s 11d. To avoid tedious in parenthesis decimal equivalents, this contemporary 1971 conversion chart has been reproduced

APPENDIX G
BIBLIOGRAPHY

Railways of Great Britain and Ireland 2nd edition
F.Wishaw 1842

History and Description of the Great Western Railway
J.C. Bourne 1846 (Reprinted David & Charles 1969)

Official Illustrated Guide to the Great Western Railway
G. Meason 1852–90 Various editions

History of the Great Western Railway (Being the story of the Broad Gauge)
G.A. Sekon 1895

History Of the Great Western Railway   Vol 1   1833–1863   1927
E.T. McDermott   Vol 2   1863–1921   1931
(Revised C.R. Clinker 1964) Ian Allan

History of the Great Western Railway   Vol 3   1923–47
O.S. Nock 1967 Ian Allan

Locomotive and Train Working in the latter part of the 19th Century Vol 4
(Reprinted from the Railway Magazine 1915–16)
E.L. Ahrens Heffer & Co, Cambridge

The Kennet and Avon Canal
Kenneth R. Clew 1968 David & Charles (USA)

Industrial Archaeology in the Bristol Region
Angus Buchanan and Neil Cossons 1969 David & Charles

The Birth of the Great Western Railway
(Extracts from the Diary and Correspondence of George Henry Gibbs)
Edited by Jack Simmons 1971 Adam and Dart (Bath) (See also GWR Magazine 1909–10)

The Rural Rides of a Bristol Churchgoer
Joseph Leech Alan Sutton 1982
(Reprint from the Bristol Times 1844)

A Gazateer of Railway Contractors and Engineers in the West of England 1830–1915
Lawrence Popplewell 1983 Melledgen Press (Ferndown, Dorset)

Track Layout Diagram of the GWR & BR(W) 2nd edition
Compiled and published by R.A. Cooke, Harwell 1988

Was your Grandfather a Railwayman?
(A Directory of Railway Archive Material for Family Historians)
Compiled and published by Tom Richards, Bristol 1988

Minutes of the Keynsham Parish Council 1894–1937

Minutes of the Keynsham Rural District Council 1894–1937
(Both at Somerset County Record Office. Both incomplete)

University of Bristol Railway Archive.
Tyndalls Park Road, Bristol

A Bibliography of British Railway History
George Ottley HMSO 1983

Bristol and Clifton Directories 1876–1900

Wrights Directories 1901–1921

Kelly's Directories

Great Western Railway Magazine 1888–1949

British Rail (Western Region) Magazine 1950–1963

Rail News (Western Region) 1963–1970

Fry's Works Magazine

Discontinued local newspapers

Felix Farley's Bristol Journal 1801–1853

Bristol Mirror 1805–1854

Bristol Times and Mirror 1865–Jan1932

Keynsham Weekly Chronicle 1946–1992
(at Wessex Newspapers, Bath)

Some other RCTS Books

LMS DIESELS
Locomotives and Railcars

Today's British motive power fleet is a tribute to the pioneering work of the LMS. Classes 56, 58, 60 and HST power cars use AC generators based on the 10800 *Hawk* development and Class 77 electrics used LMS designed bogies. Classes 40, 50 and DP2 used LMS designed engines and Peak Classes 44–46 used cab design from the famous 10000 and 10001. Our first generation diesel multiple units owe much to the 1938 80000–2 LMS railcars. And, of course, our Classes 08 and 11 bear testimony to the quality of their LMS design 60 years ago! Author Edgar Richards takes readers through the fascinating history of LMS diesel development. From the first steam conversion in 1932 to the rugged 0–6–0 shunters built in large numbers for war service at home and abroad, the revolutionary main line 10000, 10001, 10100 and 10800, and the Michelin, Coventry and LMS railcars, in total 208 locomotives, 15 railcars and 5 trolleys were operated by the LMS. Full details of their design, construction, modification, liveries, allocation and use are included.

This book includes much new material and is highly recommended.
Casebound, 219 pages, 125 illustrations.

LMS LOCOMOTIVE NAMES
The Named Locomotives of the London, Midland and
Scottish Railway and its Constituent Companies

The LNWR had a vigorous naming policy and the Midland Railway an equally determined anti-naming stance. The 1923 grouping set the stage for an absorbing battle within the management teams over naming policy with Derby's early policy success followed by Crewe's ultimate victory. Author John Goodman's absorbing read presents the full story of the LMS and its constituent companies' naming policies and the history of each named engine owned by the LMS, a total of 812. The LNWR contributed 668 of these and a complete presentation of its complex renaming system is an invaluable inclusion.
Casebound. 211 pages, 124 photographs, 25 drawings.

LMS LOCOMOTIVE DESIGN AND CONSTRUCTION
Locomotive Engineers, their Designs and Modifications

Author Arthur Cook interviewed many LMS locomotive engineers over the years to extract much new material and give a new insight into their designs' origins and performances for this book. It initiates the main part of the Society's Locomotives of the LMS series, dealing with the post-grouping era. The railway's design policies, origins and building programmes are meticulously traced with engine diagrams and modifications fully documented. An account of the development of piston valves and valve events on the LMS includes an appendix outlining the fundamentals of valve events, invaluable for preservationists.
Board covers, 175 pages, 110 illustrations.

BRITISH RAILWAYS STANDARD STEAM LOCOMOTIVES
Volume 1 Background to Standardisation and the Pacific Classes

Immediately British Railways was formed in January 1948, the railway Executive instructed Robert Riddles to design a series of standard locomotive designs. The intention was to gain material savings in running and maintenance costs by adopting as standard the best practices of the four independent companies.

In this major new series, the Society presents for the first time the complete story of British locomotive standardisation from the days of the Robinson ROD 2–8–0s to the twelve BR Standard designs totalling 999 locomotives. This book, by Paul Chancellor and Peter Gilbert, presents the Standards' design history and for each of the 66 locomotives in the popular Britannia, Duke and Clan classes its complete construction, modification, allocation and operating history.

Larger page size 212 x 272mm, Casebound, 184 pages, 151 illustrations including 17 in colour.

WESTERN CHANGE
Summer Saturdays in the West 1957–1995

Author Paul Chancellor brings almost four generations of change alive. From Halls and Granges struggling with fourteen bogies through the hydraulic and diesel electric locomotive eras to today's HSTs, traffic surveys taken by RCTS members in the Taunton, Severn Tunnel Junction, Gloucester, Bristol and Exeter areas present the changing canvas of summer Saturday railway operation. The steam to diesel transitional period is particularly featured including the temporary resurgence of steam in 1962 when diesels were transferred North. Diesel availability shortfalls and steam substitution records continue the Society's reputation for using operational detail to eloquently balance the nostalgia with realism.

Laminated cover, 169 pages, 67 illustrations including 5 maps.

LOCOMOTIVES OF THE LNER
Supplementary Information

This mammoth series has become the accredited work on the individual locomotive histories of the LNER. The first book in the series was published more than thirty years ago and since the publication date of each book much new information has been discovered.

Part 11, the nineteenth and final part of the series, presents the additional information with a relevant selection of previously unpublished photographs. An invaluable addition to the bookshelf of owners of other parts of the series.

Laminated cover, 98 pages, 85 illustrations.

RCTS Publications List

UK Post Free - Overseas add 25%   When ordering please quote PUBS 8

Title of Book	ISBN No	*Price
LMS Diesels	**0901115762**	**£19.95**
Western Change	**0901115789**	**£15.95**
BR Standard Steam Locomotives –		
Background to Standardisation and the Pacifics	**0901115819**	**£19.95**
LMS Locomotive Names	**0901115797**	**£18.95**
LMS Locomotive Design and Construction	0901115711	£16.95
Locomotives of the LNER:		
Part 2B Tender Engines B1–B19	0901115738	£13.95
Part 9A Tank Engines L1–L19	0901115401	£10.95
Part 9B Tank Engines Q1–Z5	090111541X	£10.95
Part 10A Departmental Stock, Engine Sheds,		
Boiler and Tender Numbering	0901115657	£10.95
Part 10B Railcars and Electrics	0901115665	£13.95
Part 11 Supplementary Information	**0901115800**	**£10.95**
Gt Northern Locomotive History:		
1: 1847–1866	0901115614	£12.95
2: 1867–1895	0901115746	£19.95
3A: 1896–1911	090111569X	£19.95
3B: 1911–1923	0901115703	£16.95
Highland Railway Locos 1855–1895	0901115649	£12.95
Highland Railway Locos 1895–1923	090111572X	£16.95
Shildon-Newport in Retrospect	0901115673	£10.95
Lord Carlisle's Railways	0901115436	£7.95

LOW STOCK TITLES – ORDER NOW WHILE STOCKS LAST

Locomotive History of the South Eastern Rly	0901115487	£9.90
Locos of the London, Chatham & Dover Rly	0901115479	£7.95
Locomotives of the LNER:		
Part 6B Tender Engines O1–P2	0901115541	£10.95
Part 6C Tender Engines Q1–Y10	090111555X	£10.95
Part 7 Tank Engines A5–H2	0901115134	£10.95
Locomotives of the GWR:		
Part 7 Dean's Larger Tender Engines	0901115185	£9.95
Part 8 Modern Passenger Classes	0901115193	£9.95
Part 11 Rail Motors	090111538X	£4.95

Available from: Hon. Assistant Publications Officer, Hazelhurst, Tiverton Road, Bampton, Devon, EX16 9LJ.